Teens and LGBT Issues

Christine Wilcox

Teen Well-Being

ReferencePoint
Press®

San Diego, CA

© 2016 ReferencePoint Press, Inc.
Printed in the United States

For more information, contact:
ReferencePoint Press, Inc.
PO Box 27779
San Diego, CA 92198
www.ReferencePointPress.com

Picture credits:
Cover: Thinkstock Images
Gustavo Frazao/Shutterstock.com: 10
Thinkstock Images: 17

LIBRARY OF CONGRESS CATALOGING-IN-PUBLICATION DATA

Wilcox, Christine.
　　Teens and LGBT issues / by Christine Wilcox.
　　　pages cm. -- (Compact research)
　　Audience: Grade 9 to 12.
　　Includes bibliographical references and index.
　　ISBN 978-1-60152-830-8 -- ISBN 1-60152-830-2 1. Gay youth--United States--Juvenile literature. 2. Gay rights--United States--Juvenile literature. 3. Homosexuality--Juvenile literature.
I. Title.
　　HQ76.26.W55　2016
　　362.7'8660973--dc23
　　　　　　　　　　　　　　　　　　　　　　　　　　　　　2015018385

Contents

Foreword

As modern civilization continues to evolve, its ability to create, store, distribute, and access information expands exponentially. The explosion of information from all media continues to increase at a phenomenal rate. By 2020 some experts predict the worldwide information base will double every seventy-three days. While access to diverse sources of information and perspectives is paramount to any democratic society, information alone cannot help people gain knowledge and understanding. Information must be organized and presented clearly and succinctly in order to be understood. The challenge in the digital age becomes not the creation of information, but how best to sort, organize, enhance, and present information.

ReferencePoint Press developed the *Compact Research* series with this challenge of the information age in mind. More than any other subject area today, researching current issues can yield vast, diverse, and unqualified information that can be intimidating and overwhelming for even the most advanced and motivated researcher. The *Compact Research* series offers a compact, relevant, intelligent, and conveniently organized collection of information covering a variety of current topics ranging from illegal immigration and deforestation to diseases such as anorexia and meningitis.

The series focuses on three types of information: objective single-author narratives, opinion-based primary source quotations, and facts and statistics. The clearly written objective narratives provide context and reliable background information. Primary source quotes are carefully selected and cited, exposing the reader to differing points of view, and facts and statistics sections aid the reader in evaluating perspectives. Presenting these key types of information creates a richer, more balanced learning experience.

For better understanding and convenience, the series enhances information by organizing it into narrower topics and adding design features that make it easy for a reader to identify desired content. For example, in *Compact Research: Illegal Immigration*, a chapter covering the economic impact of illegal immigration has an objective narrative explaining the various ways the economy is impacted, a balanced section of numerous primary source quotes on the topic, followed by facts and full-color illustrations to encourage evaluation of contrasting perspectives.

The ancient Roman philosopher Lucius Annaeus Seneca wrote, "It is quality rather than quantity that matters." More than just a collection of content, the *Compact Research* series is simply committed to creating, finding, organizing, and presenting the most relevant and appropriate amount of information on a current topic in a user-friendly style that invites, intrigues, and fosters understanding.

Teens and LGBT Issues at a Glance

What Does LGBT Stand For?

LGBT stands for Lesbian, Gay, Bisexual, and Transgender. It is sometimes written as LGBTQ, where *Q* is for Questioning. *Queer* is sometimes used as a synonym for LGBT.

The Difference Between Sexual Orientation and Gender Identity

Sexual orientation defines the gender that a person is sexually or romantically attracted to. Gender identity defines the gender that a person feels him- or herself to be.

What Is Transgender?

Transgender is sometimes used as an umbrella term covering a variety of gender identities. More specifically, transgender means that a person's gender identity does not match his or her biological sex. Transgender people sometimes transition to their identified gender by changing their outward appearance and, sometimes, their biological anatomy.

Other Sexual Orientations and Gender Identities

Dozens of sexual orientations and gender identities span the spectrum of what it means to be LGBT. For instance, *asexual* is a sexual orientation in which one is not attracted to any gender; *genderfluid* is a gender identity in which a person sometimes identifies as male and sometimes as female.

Why Are People LGBT?

Science does not know why people are LGBT. Some studies have indicated that a genetic component is passed on the X chromosome that may predispose people to be LGBT, but it has not been proved.

What Are the Benefits of Coming Out?

Many teens say that after they come out as LGBT they are happier and more confident—even if it means they are bullied or harassed. Teens who can own who they are feel more confident. Coming out also makes it easier to access LGBT resources, make like-minded friends, and seek help when needed.

When Coming Out Goes Badly

Sometimes parents or friends react badly to the news that a teen is LGBT. Often they need time to adjust to the idea or learn more about what it means to be LGBT. However, sometimes teens find themselves homeless after coming out to their parents. Teens should make their safety a priority when they are considering coming out.

What Is Homophobia?

Homophobia (and *transphobia*) is the irrational fear or aversion to LGBT people or behavior. *Homophobia* is also used to describe discrimination toward LGBT people.

The Effects of Homophobia

Homophobia can cause discrimination, bullying, and hate crimes against LGBT teens. The burden of dealing with homophobia can cause chronic absenteeism in school, drug and alcohol abuse, depression, self-harming behavior, and suicide.

Finding a Support System

It is crucial that LGBT teens find a support system of LGBT peers, straight allies, and trusted adults. Teens who find a community weather the effects of homophobia much more easily. Having a support system also helps teens create a strong, confident identity.

Standing Up to Discrimination

Many teens change the attitudes and social climate of their schools or community through activism and educational outreach. School gay-straight alliances (GSAs) are particularly effective in educating the student body and administration about LGBT issues.

Overview

Sexual orientation and gender identity are extremely complex aspects of the human condition. Researchers still do not fully understand why people are sexually attracted to one another or why some people identify with a gender that does not match their biology. The terminology that describes sex and gender can be equally confusing—even to the experts, who do not always agree on what each term means. In addition, the language is constantly changing as some terms fall out of favor and new ones are added. This means that some books about sex and gender issues can seem out of date as soon as they have been published.

What experts do agree upon is that individuals who have nontraditional sexual or gender identities have the right to choose how they are addressed by society. It is always a good idea to ask people what terminology they use to describe themselves rather than to make assumptions. For instance, the teen crisis intervention organization The Trevor Project notes that when people are interacting with transgender individuals (people who do not identify with their biological gender), they should "always be respectful of how someone chooses to identify, and use their preferred identity, name, and pronouns."[1] Asking how someone wishes to be addressed not only shows respect but also communicates acceptance.

What Does LGBT Stand For?

The initials LGBT stand for Lesbian, Gay, Bisexual, and Transgender. They are sometimes written as GLBT or, when only sexual orientation is being discussed, as LGB or GLB. People who describe themselves as LGBT are not implying that all four identifiers apply to them. Instead, they mean that their sexual or gender identity falls somewhere on the LGBT spectrum. Because human sexuality and gender identity are so varied and complex, the LGBT spectrum contains many more designations than the four represented in the initials LGBT, and new designations are gaining acceptance all the time.

The initials are also frequently written as LGBTQ, with the Q standing for those who are questioning their sexual or gender identity. A second Q is sometimes added to stand for *queer*, a term that is similar to LGBT in that it encompasses all nontraditional sexual and gender identities and is usually used as a synonym for LGBT.

Other initials are sometimes added to LGBT in an effort to be as inclusive as possible. For instance, some people use the initials LGBT-TQQIAAP, which stands for Lesbian, Gay, Bisexual, Transgender, Transsexual, Queer, Questioning, Intersex, Asexual, Ally, and Pansexual. Variations on the initials LGBT can get so long and complex that people refer to them as alphabet soup.

Experts have noted that today's teenagers often prefer to use language that is as specific as possible

> **Asking how someone wishes to be addressed not only shows respect but also communicates acceptance.**

to describe their sexual or gender identity rather than simply referring to themselves as LGBT or queer. As psychologists Kenneth Cohen and Ritch Savin-Williams explain, "Contemporary youths are increasingly rejecting sexual orientation identity labels (e.g., lesbian, gay, bisexual) in

When people refer to themselves as LGBT it means that they identify as lesbian, gay, bisexual, or transgender. Some experts say that today's teenagers often prefer to use even more specific language to describe their sexual or gender identity.

favor of less confining and simplistic descriptions that better represent their sexual and gender expressions, such as 'mostly straight,' 'sexually fluid,' and 'boidyke' [a boyish lesbian]."[2]

Sexual Orientation: Lesbian, Gay, and Bisexual

Sexual orientation has to do with the gender or genders that a person finds romantically and sexually attractive. It is not the same thing as sexual preference—a term that is rarely used because sexual orientation is no longer considered to be a preference or a choice by most people, including the scientific community. People who are primarily attracted to the opposite gender are referred to as *heterosexual* or *straight*. People who are primarily attracted to the same gender are referred to as *homosexual*, but because that word has taken on negative connotations, the term *gay* is usually preferred. Many gay women prefer the term *lesbian*. *Lesbian* is one of the few LGBT terms that is frequently used as a noun; it is usually acceptable to refer to a gay woman as a lesbian. However, many people do not consider it polite to use other LGBT terms as nouns because it implies that a person is defined by a single characteristic. In other words, a man who is gay should be referred to as a gay man, not as *a gay*.

The term *bisexual* (sometimes shortened to *bi*) means that a person is attracted to both men and women. Some people doubt that bisexuality is a real sexual orientation, and bisexual people can face prejudice and stigma both inside and outside of the LGBT community. "There's this idea, especially among gay men, that guys who say they're bisexual are lying, on their way to being gay, or just kind of unserious and unfocused,"[3] explains Brad Kane, a board member of the American Institute of Bisexuality (AIB). Kane identifies as a gay man but is sympathetic to the plight of bisexuals, who often have their sexuality minimized or dismissed. The AIB insists that bisexuality is not only real but is also more common than homosexuality. They point to a 2009 study published in the *Journal of Sexual Medicine* that found that 3.1 percent of American adults identified as bisexual, as compared to 2.5 percent who identified as gay or lesbian.

> **Sexual orientation is no longer considered to be a preference or a choice.**

Bisexual individuals are not necessarily attracted to men and women equally, nor are they likely to have more sexual partners or be more promiscuous than gay or straight people. Many are in monogamous relationships, either with a same sex or opposite sex partner.

Other Sexual Orientations

Dozens of other terms exist that describe sexual orientation. Many of them are paired with words that describe gender identity in an attempt to better define an individual's sexual attractions. Some terms overlap, while others are defined differently by different groups. The following is a list of a few of the more commonly used terms that relate to sexual orientation:

Asexual: Some researchers consider asexual to be a fourth major sexual orientation. People who are asexual do not experience sexual attraction or are not interested in sex. There are many degrees of asexuality and many terms that relate to it. For instance, people who are demisexual are sexually attracted only to people they know well and have an emotional connection to; they are not attracted to people they have just met or to celebrities or to the physical characteristics of strangers. People who are graysexual, on the other hand, describe themselves as in between sexual and asexual, and they rarely feel sexual attraction. The asexual community uses the umbrella term *ace* or *aces* to refer to people who are on the spectrum of asexuality.

Pansexual: For people who identify as pansexual, sexual orientation and gender identity do not figure into sexual attraction—they can potentially be attracted to anyone. Some variations on pansexual are omnisexual (finding all orientations and gender identities sexually attractive) and polysexual (attracted to more than one—but not all—orientations or identities). Polysexual should not be confused with polyamory, which is about behavior, not orientation. Polyamorous people desire to be in a relationship with more than one person at the same time—with the consent of everyone involved.

> "Some researchers consider asexual to be a fourth major sexual orientation."

Romantic orientation: Some people distinguish their sexual orientation from their romantic orientation, which can be defined as their ability to fall in love or have romantic feelings for certain types of individuals. For instance, a panromantic person can feel a romantic attraction to any person regardless of gender, while an aromantic person does not feel romantic attraction toward anyone. A woman who is sexually attracted to both men and women but who only falls in love with men might describe herself as bisexual and heteroromantic. On the other hand, she might simply describe herself as bisexual, mostly straight, or heteroflexible, or she may choose from any number of other terms she feels more accurately describes her identity.

Queer: According to the Yale University feminist magazine *Broad Recognition*, "Though 'queer' was often used in the '50s as an insult to both homosexuals and individuals who broke gender boundaries, beginning in the '90s, it underwent a massive reclamation movement."[4] *Queer* has now been reclaimed by the LGBT community and is used as an all-inclusive term for nontraditional sexual orientations and gender identities. The term is also deliberately vague, implying that the user is rejecting the labeling process altogether. As the blogger Jillian Cottle puts it, when used to describe sexual orientation, *queer* means: "My sexual orientation is unusual, and that's all I need to say about that."[5]

What Is Gender?

Even though gender and sex are sometimes used interchangeably in casual conversation, in the LGBT community they have very specific and distinct meanings. A person's sex (sometimes called their physiological or biological sex) has to do with the anatomy they are born with. A person's biological sex can be male, female, or intersex—a condition where one's anatomy is not clearly male or female. According to the Intersex Society of North America, anywhere from one in fifteen hundred to one in two thousand babies are born with reproductive or sexual anatomy that is not clearly male or female. Sometimes this is obvious at birth; other times it is discovered later in life or even after death. Some people see the intersex community as part of the LGBT community, while others believe that it should be separate.

There are other ways that gender manifests itself in humans. *Gender identity* is how individuals identify their gender internally—for instance, whether they feel male or female. As blogger Natalie Reed explains, gender identity is an innate quality. "Gender identity is not something that is concluded," she explains. "It does not have reasons. There is never a 'my gender identity is female, because X, Y and Z'. . . . There is only 'my gender identity is female.'"[6] Gender identity matches biological sex in most individuals, and they feel no internal conflict. But sometimes a person's body does not match his or her gender identity, which can cause great psychological distress.

Gender expression is a term that describes how a person behaves or expresses him- or herself in the world in relation to cultural gender concepts. For instance, in Western cultures dresses and long hair are traditionally feminine gender expressions, while neckties and short hair are traditionally masculine gender expressions. Of course, men and women have a lot of freedom in how they express their gender in today's world, and many teens experiment

> "Sometimes a person's body does not match his or her gender identity."

with different gender expressions as a way of reflecting their unique identities. However, a girl who hates to wear dresses and makeup does not necessarily feel male inside, and a boy who likes to wear eyeliner does not necessarily feel female. Plenty of people like to defy traditional gender expressions for a variety of reasons—such as for comfort, for fashion, to make a political statement, or just for fun.

Unlike gender identity, gender expression is largely under an individual's control—even though some gender expressions feel much more natural than others. For instance, some boys naturally have feminine mannerisms and some girls naturally have masculine mannerisms. To avoid being harassed or made fun of by others, they may consciously adopt a gender expression that matches their sex. This may not feel natural, but it is possible. On the other hand, most experts agree it is not possible to change one's gender identity, and attempting to do so invariably causes psychological distress.

> People who identify themselves as nonbinary may see themselves as somewhere between male and female, or they may see themselves as genderless, or as belonging to a third gender.

People whose biological sex matches their gender identity or expression are said to be cisgender or cis (*cis* means on the same side). People whose biological gender does not match their gender identity or expression are said to be transgender or trans (*trans* means on the other side).

Historically, gender has been thought of as a binary system, which means that there are only two options: male and female. (Sexual orientation was also once thought of as a binary system, with the only options being heterosexual and homosexual.) However, many people in the LGBT community reject the notion that gender is binary. People who identify themselves as nonbinary may see themselves as somewhere between male and female, or they may see themselves as genderless, or as belonging to a third gender. Some even feel that they belong to both genders and switch back and forth between masculine and feminine.

Gender Identities and Terminology

There are many terms that describe gender identity. As with terms that describe sexual orientation, some gender identity terms overlap, and some groups define the same terms in different ways. The following is a list of a few of the terms that are more commonly used:

Transgender: The gender identity with which most people are familiar is transgender. Transgender is sometimes written as trans, or trans*, the asterisk representing the variety of gender identities that are sometimes grouped under the umbrella of the one term.

A transgender person does not identify with his or her biological sex. Some transgender people feel a strong need to transition, or change their gender expression to match their gender identity. For example, a person who was born with male anatomy but has transitioned now lives as a female in society. That person often adapts a feminine name, refers to herself with feminine pronouns, and takes on the physical appearance of a woman. She may refer to herself as a transwoman, a trans girl, or simply a woman or a girl. She may or may not have undergone hormone treatment or sex reassignment surgery, but if she has, she may refer to herself as a transsexual.

However, it is not necessary to change one's anatomical sex to transition, and many transgender persons do not feel the need to undergo surgery or hormone treatment. As singer Charice Pempengco explained after she adapted a masculine appearance, "Basically my soul is male, but I'm not going to go through that stage where I'm going to change . . . my body. . . . [I'll] cut my hair and wear boy clothes and everything, but that's all."[7]

Being transgender does not have anything to do with one's sexual orientation. Transgender people can be any sexual orientation. Sexual orientation can stay the same after one transitions, or it can change—it all depends on the individual.

Agender/genderless/neutrosis: A person who identifies as agender or genderless does not identify with being either male or female. A person who identifies as neutrosis identifies with a third gender and describes that gender as neutral.

Androgynous, bigender, and trigender/polygender/pangender: A person who identifies as androgynous has one gender, but that gender is a mixture of male and female. A bigender person has two genders. Those genders may or may not include male and female. People who identify as trigender, polygender, or pangender have more than two genders. (*Tri* means three, *poly* means many, and *pan* means all.)

Genderfluid and genderqueer: People who are genderfluid switch gender identities or experience gender as a fluid, changeable state. Like the term *queer*, *genderqueer* simply means that one's gender is not cisgender. People usually use the term because either their gender identity is not easily defined or because they do not feel the need to define it. *Genderqueer* is also an umbrella term that can be used to describe all noncisgender identities.

Cross-dressing: People who cross-dress enjoy dressing in the clothes of the opposite gender but do not necessarily have a transgender identity. The term *cross-dressing* is preferable to *transvestite* or *cross-dresser* because cross-dressing is a gender expression, not a gender identity. People who cross-dress can be any sexual orientation. A drag queen is a man—often a gay man—who cross-dresses to create an exaggeratedly feminine persona as a form of performance art. Some of these artists consider the term *drag queen* to be a description of their gender identity.

How Do Teens Know If They Are LGBT?

Many people know from a very young age that they are LGBT. These people usually put a name to their feelings in their early teens. Others begin to explore their sexual or gender identities when they hit puberty, while still others do not realize they are LGBT until they are much older.

Teens who are not sure if they are LGBT are said to be questioning. Questioning one's sexual orientation or gender identity can be a long, complicated process, and some people never really come to terms with their sexual or gender identity. For others, that identity can change as they mature—sometimes many times. Some teens feel comfortable identifying as gay or straight even though they also have some same sex or opposite sex attractions, or they may feel comfortable identifying as cisgender even though they recognize that their gender identity is not that straightforward. Other teens identify more strongly with LGBT identities and ultimately decide to come out—at least to themselves—as

> " **People who cross-dress can be any sexual orientation.** "

Hundreds of organizations exist specifically to help LGBT teens with the issues they face. Building a strong group of LGBT friends and trusted adult allies is also a good way to find support.

something other than straight or cisgender. The key is that teens should feel comfortable with their identities. Finding one's sexual orientation or gender identity is about being true to oneself.

What Issues Do LGBT Teens Have About Coming Out?

The term *coming out* means announcing one's sexual orientation or gender identity to others. People usually come out many times—to family, to friends, to peers at work or school. Because most people do not know much about being transgender, people who are trans often find that coming out usually involves explaining—and sometimes justifying—their gender identity.

Teens sometimes get a negative reaction when they come out, especially from their parents. Some people think that teens are not mature enough to know if they are LGBT. Others are frightened of the homophobic reaction of others. Sometimes teens are rejected by their parents and end up homeless. However, there are great benefits to coming out. Not having to hide one's true identity is empowering, and most LGBT teens say coming out was a huge relief—regardless of the reaction they received.

What Challenges Do LGBT Teens Face?

Even though it has never been a better time to be an LGBT teen, queer teens face many challenges. They can face homophobia at home, at school, at church, or in their community. Teens whose parents reject their identities are at great risk for drug abuse, depression, and suicide.

Bullying and harassment are other serious challenges faced by LGBT teens. A 2013 national survey of LGBT teens found that bullying was the second most important problem in LGBT teens' lives, after rejection by their parents. To compare, the most important problem faced by non-LGBT teens was schoolwork and grades.

How Can Teens Get Help with LGBT Issues?

Awareness of LGBT issues has increased dramatically in recent times, and there are literally hundreds of organizations designed to help LGBT teens with the issues they face. Teens are also encouraged to build a strong support group of LGBT friends and trusted adult allies.

> **Finding one's sexual orientation or gender identity is about being true to oneself.**

Serving the LGBT community is also an excellent way to build confidence and create a strong identity. Some teens may want to improve life for LGBT students at their schools by forming a GSA. Others may work with local LGBT groups in their communities or get involved in political activism. Still other teens use the Internet to reach out to other LGBT teens who may need advice or support.

People who identify as LGBT are extremely diverse, and multiple communities make up the rainbow of sexual orientations and gender identities. Teens who are struggling with issues related to being LGBT are encouraged to reach out to those communities for advice and support. With so many LGBT organizations and resources available online, help is literally just a few clicks away.

How Do Teens Know If They Are LGBT?

66In my last year of high school I confided to a close male friend . . . that I was bisexual. . . . Somehow, 'bi-sexual' didn't sound nearly as bad as 'gay,' and I really wasn't ready to acknowledge to myself or the world the truth about my feelings.99

—Eric Marcus, an American author who writes about gay issues.

66[In high school] I didn't really understand what it meant to be a lesbian, and the thought scared me. Lesbians were something we made fun of.99

—Kathy Belge, an author and former director of the Sexual and Gender Minority Youth Resource Center in Portland, Oregon.

It is well accepted in the medical community that being LGBT is not a choice. Virtually every health care group in the United States agrees that being lesbian, gay, bisexual, or transgender is not under an individual's control. Furthermore, enough stigma is associated with being LGBT that many people argue that few would choose an LGBT identity. According to neurologist Dean Burnett, it is hard to imagine that teens "see the oppression, the suicide rates, the discrimination and harassment, the inequality, the increased risk of mental health issues, or abandonment from your family; they see all of this and think 'I gotta get me some of that'?" As Burnett explains, "This seems, to put it mildly, unlikely."[8]

So if it is not a choice, why are some people LGBT? No one knows for sure, but scientists have some theories. Recently, researchers have sought a biological cause, such as genetic influences and exposure to hormones before birth. In 1993 molecular biologist Dean Hamer was the first to find an association between homosexuality and genes on the X chromosome, which is passed on by the mother. Researchers J. Michael Bailey and Alan Sanders reported that they found a similar association in a paper published in 2014 in the journal *Psychological Medicine*. Still, scientists doubt that a single gene causes people to be LGBT, though there may be a combination of genes and other biological influences that predisposes a person to being LGBT. At this point science cannot provide an answer.

Being LGBT is not a choice.

When Do People Know They Are LGBT?

While most people realize that they are LGBT in their teen years, many have felt since they were very young that something was different about their identity. Author W. Blue, who writes an advice column on LGBT issues, remembers confusing feelings that she had at six years old after watching a movie starring Brandon Lee.

> I remember visualizing myself in a tuxedo, my arms wrapped around the waist (I guess) of a woman in a dress. I remember feeling unsettled about possibly having no choice but to become a man, if this was how I wanted to dance, and I remember thinking that becoming a man was a better option than having to kiss one. I remember liking how the woman looked in the dress, and I remember wondering what it would feel like to have her look at me the way Brandon Lee's love interest looked at him, her fingers linked behind my neck as we stared into each other's eyes meaningfully.[9]

People like Blue who have an early awareness of their sexuality or gender identity often do not put a name to these feelings until they reach their teen years. Other people do not become attracted to the same sex or identify with a different gender until they are teenagers, and still others do not realize that they are LGBT until later in life.

In addition, because there are so many different kinds of sexuality and gender identities, many teens who feel different are confused about what to call themselves. The GLBT (Gay, Lesbian, Bisexual, Transgender) National Help Center notes that many people call their help line with questions about how to label themselves. "With so much 'grey area' running between each label, it can be hard to identify just what we are feeling,"[10] they explain.

When Society Labels People LGBT

Some teens worry that they might be gay or bisexual because other people say that they are. They may be teased or bullied at school because they are perceived to be gay or because someone started a rumor about them. People experiencing this should remember that sexual orientation has nothing to do with appearance, nonsexual behavior, or conforming to gay stereotypes (for instance, the stereotypes that gay men like show tunes or lesbians like sports). As the GLBT National Help Center states, "The only thing that determines whether anyone is gay is whether or not that person is primarily physically and/or romantically attracted to people of the same gender."[11]

Gender identity is a bit more complex. The only thing that can determine gender identity is how a person chooses to define him- or herself. People are not transgender unless they say they are—regardless of how they look or act. For instance, twenty-two-year-old Ashley Wylde dresses in stereotypical masculine clothes, and after she cut her hair short, she was often mistaken for a boy. "They were putting me inside a box that I didn't feel like I belonged in," she says of the experience. "They were saying you look like a boy . . . so you must want to be a boy. . . . And I didn't. And I still don't."[12] Ashley is a lesbian, but her gender identity is female. "I prefer female pronouns, will not seek any kind of reassignment surgeries or hormone treatments, and am comfortable inside my body,"[13] she says on her blog. Teens in similar situations should remember that they are the only ones who can decide how to label themselves or what gender identity feels right.

> " Sexual orientation has nothing to do with appearance, nonsexual behavior, or conforming to gay stereotypes. "

The Spectrum of Sexual Orientation

In 1948 biologist Alfred Kinsey collected a massive amount of data about sexuality. He was among the first to conclude that sexual orientation is not binary and that people are not either homosexual or heterosexual; instead, there are many shades of gray between the two. Kinsey developed a scale that measured a person's place on the sexual orientation spectrum, with zero being exclusively heterosexual and six being exclusively homosexual. He found that only about 4 percent of men and 1 to 3 percent of women were exclusively homosexual throughout their lives, and that 50 percent were exclusively heterosexual. However, 46 to 48 percent were either aroused by both sexes or had been sexually active with both sexes—regardless of what labels they used to identify themselves. Many of these people identified as straight and were in long-term relationships with opposite sex partners.

> Teens . . . should remember that they are the only ones who can decide how to label themselves or what gender identity feels right.

More recently, researchers have found that sexual orientation may be much more complex than even Kinsey's spectrum implies. For instance, in a study of the sexual responses of college-aged males who identified as bisexual, the subjects' arousal responses did not always match how they identified themselves or lived their lives. For example, one bisexual man tested exclusively homosexual in a lab setting, while another tested as exclusively heterosexual—yet both had fulfilling relationships with both sexes.

This surprised researchers—but it may not surprise many teens today. According to sociologist Eric Anderson, young people are far more comfortable with a blurred and fluid definition of sexuality than older generations. "When I interview young men about their identity, I hear a lot of, 'I'm mostly straight,' or 'I hookup with a guy every once in a while,'" Anderson says. The young men he interviews usually identify as straight instead of bisexual—in fact, they are not sure what qualifies as bisexual. However, as Anderson explains, "They're not in a rush to put a label on that uncertainty."[14]

Deciphering Sexual Orientation

Experts encourage teens who are questioning their sexual orientation to talk to a trusted friend or a counselor who specializes in sexual orientation issues (such as those at the GLBT National Help Center's toll-free hotline). They also encourage teens to do research and to read the stories of others who have come out as lesbian, gay, or bisexual.

Psychologist Richard Reams, associate director of counseling services at Trinity University in Texas, created a web-based guide entitled *"Am I Gay?" A Guide for People Who Question Their Sexual Orientation*. In it, Reams suggests taking an evidence-based approach to answering the question and explains how to examine thoughts, feelings,

> **Young people are far more comfortable with a blurred and fluid definition of sexuality than older generations.**

and behaviors. The process he describes is not an objective test; rather, it is a way to clarify thoughts and feelings. Once people work through the questions and come to a conclusion about their sexual orientation, Reams says,

> Regardless of your understanding of your sexual orientation, you are free to describe your sexuality to yourself and to others in whatever way that makes sense to you. There are many possibilities, including straight, mostly straight, bisexual, mostly gay, mostly lesbian, gay, lesbian, queer, pansexual, "it depends on the person," etc. And you are free to revise your description of your sexual orientation in the future. Alternatively, you may decide to reject all sexual orientation identity labels.[15]

Reams also notes that younger people or people without much sexual experience may simply need to gather more evidence before coming to a conclusion about their sexual orientation. He suggests to these people, "Be patient and allow yourself as much time as you need to gather sufficient evidence about your emotional and physical attractions."[16]

Deciphering Gender Identity

According to gender therapist Dara Hoffman-Fox, people who ask the question, "Am I transgender?" usually are feeling some discomfort about the way their gender identity and their biological sex align. She suggests teens explore this discomfort with someone knowledgeable about gender identities, such as a gender identity therapist. If that is not possible, she suggests seeking out a trusted friend. Discussing the issue with someone else often helps bring clarity.

She also suggests that teens work through the book *My Gender Workbook* by Kate Bornstein. Though published in 1998, it contains insightful exercises to help teens work through complex gender identity issues. She advises teens to not get distracted by their fears and uncertainties and to "keep returning to your truth and where you want to take that. That's what really counts in the end."[17]

Coming to Terms with Being LGBT

The first stages of exploring their sexual orientation or gender identity can be a frightening time for many teens. Teens who suspect they might be LGBT sometimes choose to put off exploring their identity until they have more information—until they are sexually active, for instance. There is nothing wrong with taking time to figure out one's identity; however, having overwhelming feelings of fear and dread about being LGBT should be dealt with as soon as possible. Teens who do not deal with these feelings are at risk of developing a host of problems such as mental health issues, drug and alcohol dependence, eating disorders, and self-harming behaviors.

> **Overwhelming feelings of fear and dread about being LGBT should be dealt with as soon as possible.**

In many cases teens are afraid of being LGBT because they know it means that they will lose their heterosexual privilege—the benefits that straight people enjoy in society. Some examples of heterosexual privilege include being able to show affection in public or openly talk about one's partner without having to consider the consequences, expecting society to view your relationships as healthy and normal, not having to educate those you meet about sexual orientation or gender identity issues, and not being at risk of being confronted with homophobia or anti-LGBT violence. Transgender teens can lose far more societal privilege because their status as LGBT is sometimes much more visible.

Teens who are coming to terms with being LGBT can also feel internalized homophobia—feelings of self-hatred or self-loathing about one's LGBT identity and a strong desire to change it. Experts suggest that teens confront internalized homophobia with education. Reading widely about being LGBT is a great place to start. Openly

> Conversion therapy can lead to serious mental health issues.

gay or gay-positive therapists can also help teens work through the complicated feelings that go along with coming to terms with one's LGBT identity. According to the mental health website HealthyPlace.com, "It's critical to positively deal with internalized homophobia as its presence can prevent people from seeking appropriate healthcare, having intimate partners and living full and happy lives, and increase their risk of developing mental illness such as a substance use or an eating disorder."[18]

Conversion Therapy

One thing that experts do not suggest is that teens undergo conversion therapy. Also called reparation therapy, conversion therapy is a controversial form of therapy intended to help people change their sexual orientation or gender identity. Conversion therapy techniques can include aversion therapy (such as shocking or otherwise harming a person), intense counseling, and prayer. A 2007 study by the American Psychological Association (APA) concluded, "It is unlikely that individuals will be able to reduce same-sex attractions or increase other-sex sexual attractions"[19] through conversion therapy.

Conversion therapy can lead to serious mental health issues, and many states either have banned or are working to ban offering the therapy to minors. In response to the 2014 suicide of Leelah Alcorn, a seventeen-year-old transwoman who had been forced by her family to undergo conversion therapy, various groups have started petitions to pass a national law that would make conversion therapy on minors illegal. In 2015 President Barack Obama stated that he would support the passage of such a law.

Coming Out to Yourself

Some teens who struggle with their sexual orientation or gender identity will eventually conclude that they are indeed LGBT. This is sometimes called "coming out to yourself"—and it can be an important moment in the life of an LGBT teen. When a teen accepts being LGBT, he or she is taking the first step in forging a strong, confident personal identity. As gay activist John Paul Brammer states, "When you accept yourself, you empower yourself, and no one's opinion can take that from you."[20]

Primary Source Quotes*

How Do Teens Know If They Are LGBT?

❝I'm more drawn to men than women. But the more-than-platonic feelings I had for women . . . were real. Gay men don't have these feelings, so in that one . . . way, I am different from gay men. I'm bi.❞

—Nathaniel Frank, "Bisexuality Is Really Not That Complicated," *Slate*, March 28, 2014. www.slate.com.

Frank is the director of the What We Know Project at Columbia Law School and is writing a book about the history of marriage equality.

❝I dated [women] a fair amount. I didn't really feel like, 'I'm a liar and I'm gay and I'm doing this and I wish I wasn't.' But I did feel like it wasn't clicking like it was supposed to.❞

—Neil Patrick Harris, interview by Oprah Winfrey, *Neil Patrick Harris and David Burtka's Past Relationships with Women*, video, Oprah's Next Chapter, June 3, 2012. www.oprah.com.

Harris is an American actor and entertainer who came out as gay in 2006.

* Editor's Note: While the definition of a primary source can be narrowly or broadly defined, for the purposes of Compact Research, a primary source consists of: 1) results of original research presented by an organization or researcher; 2) eyewitness accounts of events, personal experience, or work experience; 3) first-person editorials offering pundits' opinions; 4) government officials presenting political plans and/or policies; 5) representatives of organizations presenting testimony or policy.

Primary Source Quotes

❝I knew when I was five. I was in grade school and I saw this girl and . . . it felt special. And when I was ten I was like, 'Oh! That's it, I'm gay.' I found the word.❞

—Charice Pempengco, interview by Oprah Winfrey, *Charice's Coming-Out Story: "My Soul Is Male,"* video, Oprah Where Are They Now?, October 19, 2014. www.oprah.com.

Pempengco is a twenty-two-year-old Filipina singer and actor who came out as a lesbian in 2013.

❝I did not come to the conclusion that I am a woman because I like men, jewelry, make-up, dresses and My Little Pony. I was a woman first.❞

—Natalie Reed, "Gender Expression Is Not Gender Identity," *Sincerely, Natalie*, blog, March 21, 2012. http://freethoughtblogs.com.

Reed is a transwoman and a transfeminist blogger who writes about gender and LGBT issues at FreeThoughtBlogs.com.

❝Within gay and lesbian communities bisexuality is often figured as a 'phase' or 'cover' for a 'truer' gay or lesbian identity.❞

—Jonathan Alexander and Serena Anderlini-D'Onofrio, "Bisexuality and Queer Theory: An Introduction," in Jonathan Alexander and Serena Anderlini-D'Onofrio, eds., *Bisexuality and Queer Theory: Intersections, Connections and Challenges*. New York: Taylor & Francis, 2012. Kindle edition.

Alexander and Anderlini-D'Onofrio teach and write about LGBT issues. Alexander is a professor of English at the University of California, Irvine, and Anderlini-D'Onofrio is a professor of humanities at the University of Puerto Rico.

❝Gay identity is a Western construct. In other cultures, men can have penetrative sex with other men without it meaning that they are gay.❞

—Karine Igartua, "Identity Problem," in Petros Levounis, Jack Drescher, and Mary Barber, eds., *LGBT Casebook*. Arlington, VA: American Psychiatric Publishing, 2012, p. 259.

Igartua is codirector of the McGill University Sexual Identity Centre and assistant professor of medicine at McGill University in Montreal, Quebec, Canada.

"I was about twelve when I realized what gay meant and that I had it. It felt like a disease to me. I was like, 'Oh *no*. Like life isn't hard enough.'"

—Jane Lynch, interview by Ricky Camilleri, "Actress and Comedian Jane Lynch LIVE," *Huffington Post Live*, July 9, 2014. http://live.huffingtonpost.com.

Lynch is an actor who starred in the television show *Glee*.

"In reality, it is so hard to be one hundred percent certain about something about ourselves [like gender identity]."

—Dara Hoffman-Fox, "How Do I know If I'm Transgender?," YouTube, April 24, 2014. https://www.youtube.com/watch?v=Oea10Q5tG4Q.

Hoffman-Fox is a licensed professional counselor and gender therapist who identifies as genderfluid.

"Late into my last year of high school, Nicolosi [my therapist] had a final conversation with my parents and told them that the [conversion therapy] treatment had been a success. . . . A few weeks later, our housekeeper caught me with a boy in our backyard."

—Gabriel Arana, "My So-Called Ex-Gay Life," *American Prospect*, April 11, 2012. http://prospect.org.

Arana, the senior editor at the *American Prospect*, writes about gay rights. In college he nearly committed suicide because of the psychological damage done by conversion therapy treatment when he was a teenager.

How Do Teens Know If They Are LGBT?

- A 2009 study published in the *Journal of Sexual Medicine* reported that **3.1 percent of American adults** identified as bisexual, while **2.5 percent** identified as gay or lesbian.

- In a 2013 Pew Research Survey, only **28 percent** of people who identified as bisexual said they were open about it.

- The 2013 Pew Research Survey also found that **74 percent of LGBT individuals** do not want to be seen as different because of their LGBT identity.

- Psychologist Walter Bockting reported in 2008 that **among trans-women 27 percent** are attracted to men, **35 percent** are attracted to women, and **38 percent** are attracted to men and women.

- Bockting also found that **among transmen 10 percent** are attracted to men, **55 percent** are attracted to women, and **35 percent** are attracted to men and women.

- A 2005 study by the National Center for Health Statistics found that **among teens aged 15–19, 2.4 percent of males and 7.7 percent of females** reported having had same-sex sexual contact in the previous twelve months.

The Four LGB Identities

The diagram below illustrates what psychiatrist Jack Drescher calls the four gay identities. "Closeted" individuals are either concealing or are in denial (dissociation) about their same-sex attractions. "Homosexually self-aware" individuals are able to acknowledge their same-sex attractions, at least to themselves, though they may not want them or act on them. People who identify as "lesbian, gay, or bisexual" have accepted this identity. And people who are "nongay" have rejected the LGB identity and seek to change it. C. Dresher suggests that many LGB people experience all four of these identities at some point.

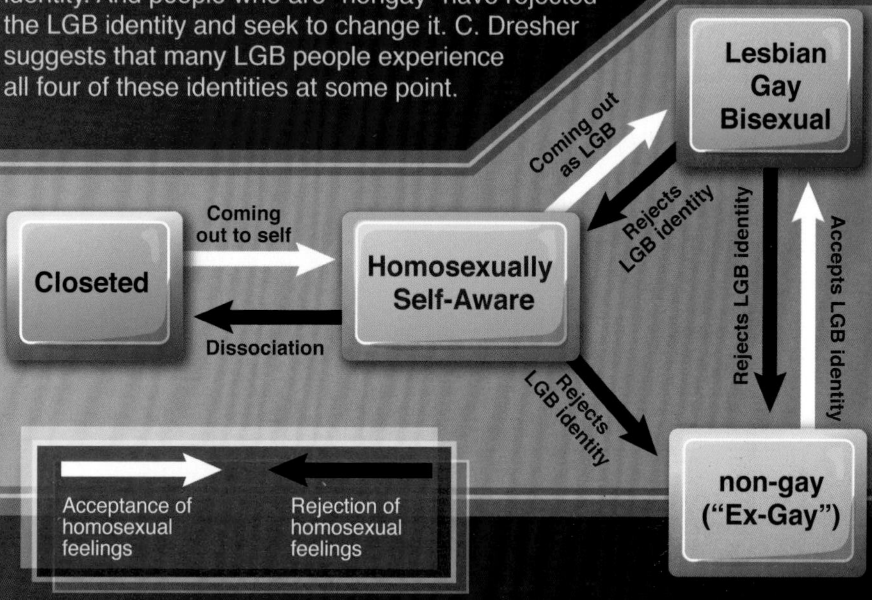

Closeted

Coming out to self

Dissociation

Homosexually Self-Aware

Coming out as LGB

Rejects LGB identity

Lesbian Gay Bisexual

Rejects LGB identity

Accepts LGB identity

Rejects LGB identity

non-gay ("Ex-Gay")

Acceptance of homosexual feelings

Rejection of homosexual feelings

Source: Jack Drescher, "What's in Your Closet?," in Petros Levounis, Jack Drescher, and Mary Barber, eds., *LGBT Casebook*, Arlington, VA: American Psychiatric Publishing, 2012, p. 9.

- In Native American culture, "two spirit" people are individuals who identify with both a male and female gender.

- The Hijra people of India represent a third gender, which is recognized by Indian law.

The Kinsey Scale

The Heterosexual-Homosexual Rating Scale was developed by Alfred Kinsey in 1948 in response to his discovery that people were not exclusively heterosexual or homosexual. Though most of the thousands of people he interviewed reported being exclusively heterosexual, many admitted to sexual thoughts or behaviors that were same-sex oriented. A percentage of homosexual individuals also disclosed opposite sex attractions. While other researchers have since built on Kinsey's research, many people still refer to the Kinsey Scale when describing their own sexual orientation.

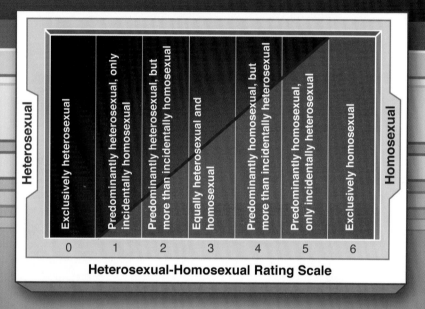

Source: The Kinsey Institute, "Kinsey's Heterosexual-Homosexual Rating Scale," 2015. www.kinseyinstitute.org.

- According to Yale historian John Boswell, records of same-sex relationships have been found in nearly every culture throughout history, with varying degrees of acceptance.

- The National Museum & Archive of Lesbian and Gay History estimates that **1 percent** of the US population are transsexuals.

Education Affects Whether Americans Think Being Gay Is a Choice

A 2013 poll found that Americans are split over whether people are born gay or lesbian or choose their sexual orientation. However, when the education of those polled is taken into account, the more educated responders tend to say that people who are gay or lesbian are born that way—a point of view that is confirmed by the vast majority of medical and psychological experts.

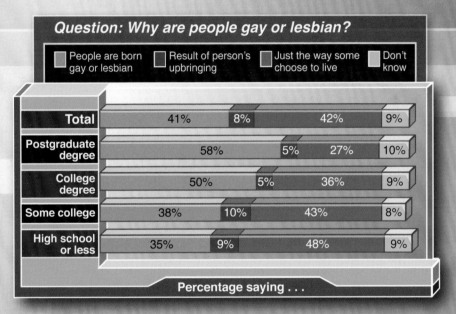

Question: Why are people gay or lesbian?

	People are born gay or lesbian	Result of person's upbringing	Just the way some choose to live	Don't know
Total	41%	8%	42%	9%
Postgraduate degree	58%	5%	27%	10%
College degree	50%	5%	36%	9%
Some college	38%	10%	43%	8%
High school or less	35%	9%	48%	9%

Percentage saying . . .

Source: David Masci, "Americans Are Still Divided on Why People Are Gay," Pew Research Center, March 6, 2015. www.pewresearch.org.

- According to geneticist Barry Starr, if one identical twin is gay, the other has about a **20 to 50 percent** chance of being gay.

- Some African Americans prefer the term SGL (same gender loving) to LGBT.

What Issues Do LGBT Teens Have with Coming Out?

66 Tonight . . . a young person . . . will struggle to fall to sleep, wrestling alone with a secret he's held as long as he can remember. Soon, perhaps, he will decide it's time to let that secret out. What happens next depends on him. . . . But it also depends on us. 99

—President Barack Obama, the forty-fourth president of the United States, in response to the suicide of Leelah Alcorn, a seventeen-year-old transwoman who had been forced by her family to undergo religious therapy to convert her back to being a boy.

66 I didn't even go on a date or anything with a guy until I was twenty-four. . . . I immediately regretted all that time I wasted trying to fit in and be something I wasn't. 99

—Brian Gallivan, actor and comedian who came out as a gay man in his twenties. Gallivan starred in Second City's YouTube series *Sassy Gay Friend* and later created the American sitcom *The McCarthys*.

Coming out as LGBT is a significant decision. For some, the process is simple and affirming; for others, it is complex and fraught with awkwardness, rejection, and hardship. Because everyone's circumstances are different, choosing when to come out—and to whom—is a very personal decision.

What Does It Mean to "Come Out"?

The term *coming out* simply means to be open and honest about being LGBT to family, friends, or a community such as school or the workplace. Sometimes coming out happens in a casual conversation; other times it is more formal. Some people choose to tell others in a letter or text, while others just make an announcement on the Internet. However it is done, coming out is usually a significant moment in the lives of LGBT teens—it marks the point when they feel confident enough about their sexual orientation or gender identity to publicly own it, regardless of the consequences.

Many researchers talk about coming out not as a single action but as a process of increasing self-awareness. The first few steps in the process involve questioning one's identity. For teens this is often a time when they try to learn as much as they can about sexual orientation or gender identity in an attempt to put a name to how they feel. The next step involves accepting, or owning, that identity. This stage is sometimes called "coming out to oneself." It can also involve revealing one's sexual or gender identity to a small circle of people or beginning to socialize with other LGBT youth. Teens might come out to their friends during this stage but not to their parents or to most people at school. Many teens stay in this stage until they are adults because it is too risky to be openly LGBT at their home or their school.

> **Coming out is usually a significant moment in the lives of LGBT teens.**

In the final step individuals commit to their identity and live openly as LGBT. According to the LGBT website AVERT.org, people in this final stage recognize that being LGBT is "an important aspect of, 'who I am', and, 'how I want to live my life'. People develop a sense of contentment with being LGBT and see it as a valid way of life."[21] Some LGB people fall in love during this stage, while some transgender people choose to transition and live openly as their true gender.

The experience of coming out is different for everyone. Some teens—especially transgender teens—find they have to come out over and over again, explaining their identity to everyone they come in contact with. Others simply decide to live openly as LGBT without making any sort of announcement. For instance, when W. Blue was a teen she never explicitly told her parents—or anyone else—that she was a lesbian. "I never saw the point in asking others, outright, to accept my sexuality. I already looked gay enough for strangers to yell 'dyke' at me on the street, so I imagined my sexuality was pretty self-explanatory."[22]

What Are the Benefits of Coming Out?

Many teens report that they are glad that they came out—even if they did not get the response that they wanted. When people are honest and upfront about such an essential part of their identity, they often feel a huge sense of relief that they no longer have to pretend to be something they are not. After seventeen-year-old Charlotte came out as a lesbian to her parents, she said, "For once I just felt free, like a massive weight and worry were gone in an instant." To Charlotte, coming out meant, "I could finally truly be me and I didn't have to carry on hiding who I was."[23]

> **When people own their identity, they reject the idea that they should be ashamed of it.**

One reason that coming out can be an empowering experience is that when people own their identity, they reject the idea that they should be ashamed of it. Even when people are proud of their identity, it can generate feelings of shame when they are in a situation where they need to hide it.

Coming Out to Family Members

People who are nervous about coming out are probably the most apprehensive about coming out to their families. While most parents of teenagers understand what it means to be LGBT, there may be some glaring gaps in their knowledge. Many parents immediately think about the sexual part of being LGBT and become uncomfortable. They may also become concerned about the difficulties that some LGBT face, such as discrimination and gay bashing. Regardless of their preconceptions and concerns, coming out is usually an emotional experience for both parent and child. This is why most experts suggest that teens wait until they are confident about their identities before coming out to their parents—unless they have the sort of relationship where their parents can help them understand their identity.

Some decide to come out in a letter or an e-mail so that they can express their thoughts clearly in a calm state of mind. Many experts actually suggest coming out to family members in a letter because it gives everyone time to process their emotions. Many parents feel a sense of confusion and loss when their child comes out as LGBT. They have imagined a future for their child that will now be different. Parents who are asked to see their child as being a different gender may need even more time to adjust. Most of their fears can be relieved through education, but that also can take time.

Teens who do not get an immediate positive reaction should remember that it can take time for anyone to adjust to big news. As Wayne Dhesi, creator of the website R U Coming Out? says, "You should respect that [some people] may need some time to get their heads around what you tell them. Their silence or facial expressions do not mean that they don't approve, it just means that they need time to absorb what you are telling them."[24]

When Coming Out Goes Badly

Some parents reject their teen who comes out. They may simply believe that LGBT identities are wrong, or have anti-LGBT religious beliefs, or be misinformed about what LGBT identities are. Some are worried about what their friends and neighbors may think. Some simply do not believe a teen who says he or she is LGBT. As Montana, a lesbian teen, writes on the website JustLeftTheCloset.com, "When I was 12 I told my parents that I was gay, however they chose to ignore . . . that I had ever brought it up, and just to spare myself the argument and lectures . . . I never brought it up again."[25]

The Family Acceptance Project (FAP) teaches families that it is possible to support their teen even if they think being LGBT is wrong. They have found that educating family members about LGBT issues increases their understanding and acceptance. They also teach families who want to be accepting of their teens what behaviors are supportive and accepting, and which are not. "Many people think they're accepting and supportive of an LGBT adolescent but they're not," explains Caitlin Ryan, director of FAP. "They're actually ambivalent and tolerant at best."[26]

When teens are deciding whether to come out to their parents, they should carefully evaluate their safety and the likelihood that they will be told to leave the household. Safety should be a teen's primary concern. Teens are not obligated to tell their parents about their LGBT identity. If telling them may compromise their safety, they should wait until they are self-sufficient.

Coming Out at School

Whether to come out at school depends on how accepting the students and the school's culture is toward LGBT students. If a school has a GSA, a strong anti-bullying policy, and a community of students who are out, teens will probably not have to worry much about their safety or about discrimination from the administration. However, if a school's culture is anti-LGBT, teens may want to share their LGBT identity with only a few trusted friends. Bullying and harassment can have devastating effects on a person's quality of life, mental health, and personal safety. While staying "in the closet" is never ideal, personal safety should always be a teen's primary concern.

However, if school is a safe and positive environment, experts say that teens who come out at school are generally happier than those who do not. In fact, a 2014 study published in the *American Journal of Ortho-psychiatry* found that teens who came out in high school reported higher self-esteem and life satisfaction as young adults, regardless of whether they were victimized for their LGBT identity. This research suggests that advising teens to conceal their identity to avoid bullying may not be good advice. "We know from our other studies that requiring LGBT adolescents to keep their LGBT identities secret or not to talk about them is associated with depression, suicidal behavior, illegal drug use and risk for HIV," says Ryan. "And helping them learn about and disclose their LGBT identity to others helps protect against risk and helps promote self-esteem and overall health."[27] Because bully-

> " **Safety should be a teen's primary concern.** "

ing is also associated with suicide and other risks, groups such as FAP must carefully weigh the risks and benefits when advising teens about coming out at school. Teens should do the same.

When a Teen Is "Outed" by Someone Else

Unfortunately, many LGBT teens do not have control over their coming out experience. Some of them are perceived as LGBT and may already be experiencing bullying at school. Others are outed by a friend, either accidentally or deliberately. Sixteen-year-old Jen had that experience. She writes, "A couple of years back I told one person and they spread it around the whole year. I managed to dismiss it as a rumor, but people still shoved me into lockers and slipped notes in my locker saying 'dyke.'"[28]

> **Owning one's identity increases confidence and self-esteem and can take some of a bully's power away.**

No one has the right to out anyone else. However, if this happens it may be best to simply come out. Owning one's identity increases confidence and self-esteem and can take some of a bully's power away.

Coming Out as Transgender

Teens who come out as transgender often face more resistance and opposition than teens who are LGB. Gender identity affects many areas of a person's life, and many transgender people feel that they do not have a choice about coming out. Transgendered children are coming out at younger and younger ages as understanding about gender identity grows.

For children who have supportive parents, coming out early can be a blessing. Spenser, a sixteen-year-old transgender boy, came out to his parents when he was fourteen. He had always felt like a male, and when he learned the term *transgender* he instantly identified with it. His parents immediately accepted him and began researching the best way to support him. In Spenser's case, that meant helping him transition and getting him on hormone therapy—a controversial practice that nonetheless has very positive results for transgender youth. While many doctors believe that young people should not be permitted to undergo hormone therapy because it alters normal growth and development, those who support it say that by stopping the changes in the body that occur during puberty, transgender teens have a much easier transition. Spenser also takes testosterone, which has given him a deeper voice and denser musculature. It allows him to effectively pass as male, so he does not need to come out any longer. "I've already socially transitioned and I don't feel the need to come out to everyone," he says. "I'm not ashamed to be transgender, but it's not a huge part of my life."[29]

> " [Many] transgender teens . . . must come out again and again to everyone they meet. "

Other transgender teens face much more opposition. Those who cannot easily pass for another gender must come out again and again to everyone they meet. They may also find that each time they come out, they need to explain how they know they are transgender.

Coming Out Is Not About Other People

Teens who are contemplating coming out should remember that when and how to come out is entirely their decision. Even though parents and friends may feel as though they are entitled to know, they are not. According to Planned Parenthood, "Coming out is a very personal decision. You—and only you—get to decide if and when, to whom, and how you come out. . . . Never let anyone or anything pressure you into coming out before you're ready."[30]

What Issues Do LGBT Teens Have with Coming Out?

66 My daughter—then my four-year-old son—said these words to me: 'Mom, you know I'm really a girl, right? I'm a girl on the inside.' 99

—Debi Jackson, "Debi Jackson reading 'That's Good Enough,'" YouTube, July 9, 2014.
https://www.youtube.com/watch?v=-oIuw3yIyhI.

Jackson, who describes herself as Southern Baptist Republican from Alabama, is the mother of a seven-year-old male-to-female transgender daughter named A.J.

66 I really want to be completely out. I'm sick and tired of people nagging me for not having a girl friend, for not laughing along with their gay jokes, etc. The little voice inside of me just wants to scream out at the lunch table that I'm gay and proud. 99

—Beloudstandproud, "Life: What's It Like at Your School?," forum post, JustLefttheCloset.com, March 16, 2012.
www.justleftthecloset.com.

Beloudstandproud is the screen name of a gay male teen who attends a small high school in the United States. He has been bullied about his perceived sexual orientation since junior high and is afraid that coming out publicly at school will make things worse.

* Editor's Note: While the definition of a primary source can be narrowly or broadly defined, for the purposes of Compact Research, a primary source consists of: 1) results of original research presented by an organization or researcher; 2) eyewitness accounts of events, personal experience, or work experience; 3) first-person editorials offering pundits' opinions; 4) government officials presenting political plans and/or policies; 5) representatives of organizations presenting testimony or policy.

❝Experiencing homosexual feelings can be very difficult to come to terms with, particularly if a person lacks knowledge about homosexuality or is aware of stigma attached to being gay or lesbian.**❞**

—AVERT, "Coming Out," April 14, 2015. www.avert.org.

AVERT is an international HIV and AIDS charity that works to avert HIV and AIDS worldwide in part by educating young people about sexual issues.

....

❝One of the most supportive things any parent can offer at the moment of coming out is simply a hug and reassurance that there is still a relationship based on love.**❞**

—John Sovec, "Supporting LGBTQ Teens Coming Out: It's a Family Process," GoodTherapy.org, February 12, 2015.

Sovec is a marriage and family therapist who specializes in helping LGBT teens and their families through the coming out process.

....

❝Once . . . [I came out] a light came on, on me, on the inside, around me, every[where]. I felt like I was Brittney Griner, like I was who I am now. I wasn't hiding anymore.**❞**

—Brittney Griner, "Brittney Griner Speaks About Coming Out at the #GLAADAwards," YouTube, May 13. 2013. https://www.youtube.com/watch?v=IJZddnpzUB4.

Griner was the number one WNBA draft pick in 2013 and currently plays for the Phoenix Mercury. She came out as a lesbian in the ninth grade.

....

❝When someone comes out, people's first reaction to that is not always their true reaction. Sometimes after they have had time to think about it, they either become more or less . . . supportive.**❞**

—Matt Kailey, "Ask Matt: Nowhere to Live if I Transition," *Matt Kailey's Tranifesto*, blog, March 24, 2014. http://tranifesto.com.

Kailey is a transgender man who writes and speaks about transgender issues.

....

“The pressures on gay teens can be overwhelming—to keep secrets, tell lies, deny who you are, and try to be who you're not.”

—Alex Sanchez, "Who Is Alex?" www.alexsanchez.com.

Sanchez is the author of numerous award-winning LGBT young adult novels including *Rainbow Boys*, *The God Box*, *Bait*, and *Boyfriends with Girlfriends*.

....

“At fourteen, I decided I would keep my sexual identity a secret forever.”

—Barney Frank, *Frank*. New York: Farrar, Straus and Giroux, 2015. Kindle edition.

Frank was a member of the US House of Representatives from 1981 until 2013. He decided to come out as a gay man publicly in 1987.

....

“I am tired of hiding and I am tired of lying by omission. I suffered for years because I was scared to be out. My spirit suffered, my mental health suffered, and my relationships suffered.”

—Ellen Page, Time to Thrive Conference, Las Vegas, Nevada, February 14, 2014. http://variety.com.

Page is an American actor.

....

What Issues Do LGBT Teens Have with Coming Out?

- A 2013 survey by the Pew Research Center found that only **28 percent** of people who identified as bisexual were out to the most important people in their lives.

- The Pew Research Center survey also found that **77 percent of gay men and 71 percent of lesbians were** out to the most important people in their lives.

- According to Caitlin Ryan and Donna Futterman, health care professionals and authors of *Lesbian and Gay Youth*, boys are usually aware of same sex attractions by age thirteen and girls by age fourteen to sixteen. However, boys often do not come out to themselves until age nineteen to twenty, and girls until age twenty-one to twenty-three.

- According to a study by the TransYouth Project, transgender children as young as five respond to psychological gender-association tests in the same way as cisgender children, supporting the idea that young trans children are not confused about their gender identity.

- A 2012 Gallup poll of 120,000 Americans found that **3.4 percent said yes** when asked if they were LGBT. Younger adults (aged eighteen to twenty-four) were more likely to identify as LGBT, with **8.3 percent of women and 4.6 percent of men** identifying as LGBT.

LGBT Teens Are More Likely to Be Out to Peers than to Teachers

A study published in 2014 found that LGBT teens are more likely to be out to their peers than to their teachers. A national online survey of LGBT students in grades six through twelve found that nearly 60 percent of LGBT students were out to most or all of their peers, but only about a third were out to most or all of their teachers or other school staff.

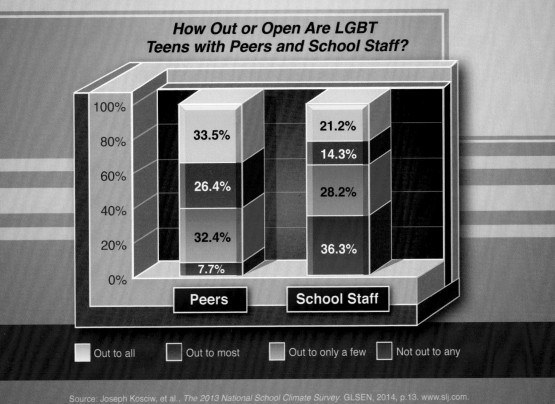

How Out or Open Are LGBT Teens with Peers and School Staff?

Source: Joseph Kosciw, et al., *The 2013 National School Climate Survey.* GLSEN, 2014, p.13. www.slj.com.

- According to a 2014 study published in the *American Journal of Orthopsychiatry*, LGBT teens who come out have higher self-esteem and lower levels of depression as young adults, regardless of whether they experience bullying.

Lack of Acceptance Prevents Teens from Coming Out

A Human Rights Campaign survey of over ten thousand LGBT youth aged thirteen to seventeen found that the top reasons teens are not out to their families or at school is that they think they will not be accepted or fear they will be treated differently or judged.

Reasons LGBT Youth Do Not Come Out

To Their Families

30%	Say their family is not accepting or is homo/bi/transphobic
19%	Say they are scared of reaction, afraid, or don't know how their family will react
16%	Say they have "religious reasons"
10%	Say they are not ready
10%	Don't or can't talk with their family

At School

31%	Say they will be treated differently or judged
26%	Say they do not see the need to come out or it is not anyone's business
9%	Say they are afraid of bullying
7%	Say their teachers and/or school are very conservative

Source: Human Rights Campaign, "Being Out: National Coming Out Day Youth Report," 2016. www.hrc.org.

- According to Caitlin Ryan of the Family Acceptance Project, the average age that people come out as LGBT had dropped from the early twenties in the 1970s to about thirteen years old in 2015.

- According to a 2013 survey by the Human Rights Campaign, **90 percent of teens** who are LGBT are out to their close friends.

Most LGB Adults Say They Came Out After Teen Years

A 2013 survey by the Pew Research Center of 1,154 LGB adults found that most lesbian, gay, and bisexual adults first suspected they were LGB at about twelve years old but did not come out to a family member or a close friend until about age twenty.

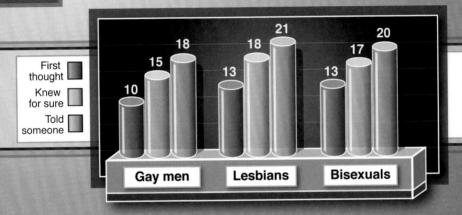

Median Age That LGB Adults First Thought, Knew for Sure, and Told Someone They Were LGB

Legend:
- First thought
- Knew for sure
- Told someone

Gay men: 10, 15, 18
Lesbians: 13, 18, 21
Bisexuals: 13, 17, 20

Source: Pew Research Center, "A Survey of LGBT Americans," June 13, 2013. www.pewsocialtrends.org.

- The Human Rights Campaign survey also found that **64 percent of LGBT high school youth** say that they are out to their classmates.

- According to the Sexuality Information and Education Council (SIEC), **25.9 percent of twelve-year-olds** said they were uncertain about their sexual orientation. That number declined to **5 percent** among seventeen-year-olds.

- A survey of 1,000 parents by Horizons Foundation in 2001 found that **76 percent of parents** nationwide would be comfortable talking to their child about issues related to LGBT issues.

- National Coming Out Day is held on October 11, the anniversary of the National March on Washington, DC, for Lesbian and Gay Rights in 1987.

What Challenges Do LGBT Teens Face?

66There's nothing wrong with you. There's a lot wrong with the world you live in.**99**

—Chris Colfer, an American actor and star of the television series *Glee*.

66Trans identities are seen as always less than, always secondary, are always expected to get out of the way for the expectations of friends and family.**99**

—Greta Martela, executive director of the help line Trans Lifeline.

A few decades ago GSAs and other pro-LGBT clubs were unheard of in schools. The word *gay* was a perfectly acceptable way to put down anyone or anything that was not cool, and few teens felt safe being out about their sexual orientation or gender identity. Today, not only are many LGBT teens accepted by their families and welcomed by their schools, they are likely to be popular—as reflected by the growing number of LGBT couples who have been voted as king and queen (or king and king or queen and queen) of their homecoming celebrations and proms.

Still, while homophobic attitudes are waning, many LGBT teens still face homophobia from their peers, discrimination from their school administrations, and rejection from their families. According to the

Human Rights Campaign survey, when LGBT teens were asked what it was like to be LGBT in their community, the most common answer was a description of intolerance. And when asked to describe one thing in their lives they would change, the number one answer was homophobia (expressed on the survey as understanding/tolerance/hate). As one survey respondent said, "It's very easy to look at me and tell I'm gay and it makes me feel afraid to walk around knowing there are people here in my hometown that hate me, and people like me, enough to attack me."[31]

What Is Homophobia?

Homophobia is defined as the "irrational fear of, aversion to, or discrimination against homosexuality or homosexuals."[32] Examples of homophobia can range from subtle bias, such as being graded more harshly by a teacher, to overt victimization such as physical assault. Homophobia against transgender people is often called transphobia.

Many people accused of homophobia insist that their feelings toward LGBT people are not irrational or fear-based. They claim instead that they simply do not agree, on moral or religious grounds, with same-sex sexual behavior or nontraditional gender identities or expressions. Because of this, it is often more productive to talk about homophobia not as an attitude but as a behavior—a negative or discriminatory action toward people who are LGBT simply because of their sexual orientation or gender identity or expression.

> When asked to describe one thing in their lives they would change, the number one answer was homophobia.

Homophobia and Gender Expression

In many cases homophobia is a reaction to a person's gender expression rather than to his or her actual sexual orientation. Many people simply assume that women who seem masculine are lesbian and men who seem feminine are gay. A lesbian who is cisgender in her gender expression will probably experience less homophobia than a transman—who may be mistaken for a lesbian.

> **Any teen whose gender expression is not strictly cisgender . . . runs the risk of encountering homophobia.**

Males who do not display culturally accepted masculine behavior or dress are at particular risk of victimization. Writer-director Jennifer Siebel Newsom, creator of the film *The Mask We Live In*, which examines how male gender roles affect boys, says that society teaches people "to devalue the feminine, not just in others but in ourselves. . . . So many young men, even if they're not gay, they're bullied because they're earnest and that's associated with femininity."[33] Other characteristics that are associated with femininity are emotion, expressiveness, or affection toward the same sex. Because of this, any teen whose gender expression is not strictly cisgender, regardless of whether he or she is LGBT, runs the risk of encountering homophobia.

What Causes Homophobia?

The causes of homophobia are varied. Some people are homophobic because their parents are homophobic. Others have been told that being LGBT is deviant or unnatural or that all LGBT people are promiscuous. Many people are taught by their religion that LGBT behavior is contrary to the will of God. (Critics point out that there are plenty of ideas in religious texts that violate basic human rights—including the idea that a woman is the property of her husband.)

One popular theory is that people who are homophobic are secretly afraid of being LGBT. According to the authors of *"You Can Tell Just by Looking": And 20 Other Myths About LGBT Life and People*, this is usually not true. "Rather than homophobes repressing their homosexual feelings, it is more likely that they are avoiding the idea of homosexuality"[34]—a concept that may make them uncomfortable. Still, the authors acknowledge that several studies have shown that people who are suppressing same-sex attractions do tend to express more homophobic attitudes than those who are not.

Homophobia at Home

In 2014 twenty-year-old Daniel Ashley Pierce was kicked out of his home for being gay. He recorded a conversation he had with his parents and posted it online, where it quickly went viral. A woman who may be his stepmother or grandmother can be heard saying the following:

> You can deny it all you want to, but I believe in the word of God and God creates nobody that way. It's a path that you have chosen. . . . [Because] you have chosen that path, we will not support you any longer. You will need to move out and find wherever you can to live and do what you want to because I will not let people believe that I condone what you do.[35]

The exchange quickly escalated to verbal abuse, and Pierce said he was hit repeatedly in the face by his stepmother. People were shocked by the hatred expressed by the family. As one online commenter said, "This made me cry. Now I'm even more frightened to come out to my parents as pan/bi."[36]

LGBT teen homelessness is a significant problem. While only about 5 percent of teens are LGBT, up to 40 percent of homeless teens are LGBT. And because teens are coming out at younger and younger ages, the risks they face while homeless increase. At the same time, most major cities have seen cuts in funding to homeless shelters, and they often do not have the resources to keep LGBT homeless teens safe. *NBC News* reports that there are only 4,000 beds available in the United States for homeless young adults, and only 350 of them are set up for LGBT teens, who are at greater risk of harassment and assault. Shelters that do not have facilities for teens often have to turn them away, and teens are left to fend for themselves on the streets. According to Lost-n-Found, a homeless center for LGBT teens in Atlanta, Georgia, "There are only about 48 hours from the time a kid becomes homeless before 33 percent of youth begin to engage in risky behaviors as theft, drug activity or selling their bodies for money to survive."[37]

> " Because teens are coming out at younger and younger ages, the risks they face while homeless increase. "

Some LGBT teens leave home voluntarily after coming out to their families because they feel rejected. But even if they stay, the lack of acceptance and support from their families still can put them at risk. A study by FAP found that young people who are rejected by their families are three times as likely to use illegal drugs, almost six times as likely to be depressed, and more than eight times as likely to have attempted suicide.

Why Do Parents Reject Their LGBT Children?

According to Caitlin Ryan, regardless of whether parents are accepting or rejecting of their LGBT teen, "underneath they feared what might happen to their child in a homophobic and transphobic world."[38] Even though society has become much more accepting of LGBT individuals in recent years, nearly all LGBT teens will face some level of homophobia and discrimination. Some parents may also worry that their children will lose the heterosexual privilege and sense of inclusion that straight and cisgender people typically enjoy in society. According to Ryan, these concerns are often expressed as criticism, a rejection of a teen's LGBT identity, or an insistence that the teen change.

> " **Young people bully in order to increase their social standing.** "

Many parents later regret their reaction to their child's sexual orientation or gender identity. "We found that many families whose children were homeless and on the street wished that they had done something differently, that they hadn't reacted out of anger," Ryan explains. "This included families that were very religiously and culturally conservative. . . . They learned about LGBT issues and became more supportive over time. Sometimes it was too late and some of them had never seen their child again."[39]

Homophobia at School

Many school districts have adopted policies to make school a safe space for LGBT students. However, homophobia and bullying of LGBT students is still a serious problem in many parts of the United States. A nationwide survey of students between the ages of thirteen and twenty-one found that over half of LGBT students felt unsafe at school. In addition, 74.1 percent of LGBT students were verbally harassed and 36.2

were physically harassed at their schools. According to the Gay, Lesbian, & Straight Education Network (GLSEN), "Feeling unsafe or uncomfortable at school can negatively affect the ability of students to thrive and succeed academically, particularly if it results in avoiding school."[40] They found that nearly one-third of LGBT students missed a day of school, and over one-tenth missed four or more days over the past month because they felt unsafe or uncomfortable.

> **Private schools . . . can legally deny enrollment to students for being LGBT.**

Studies of bullying behavior have found that young people bully in order to increase their social standing among their peer groups. Bullies will often pick an easy target, and since teens who are perceived as LGBT also are sometimes isolated, they can be easy targets. For this reason, homophobia may not be the primary motivation for bullying in many cases. While knowing this may not help prevent bullying, it may reduce some of the feelings of shame that bullying can sometimes provoke.

When School Administrations Condone Homophobia

The GLSEN survey found that of the LGBT students who reported harassment, 61.6 percent said their school's administration did nothing in response. In addition, more than 51.4 percent of students reported hearing homophobic remarks from their teachers or other school staff. The attitude of the administration toward its LGBT students can have more subtle effects as well. Some administrations invalidate the LGBT experience by eliminating any references to it. The survey found that less than half of students could find information about LGBT-related issues in their school libraries or online via their school computers, and that less than one-fifth had been exposed to positive representations of LGBT people or history in class.

In some religious schools homophobia is codified into school policy. At Lutheran High North in Houston, Texas, that policy states that the school can discontinue enrollment of any student who is found to be "participating in, promoting, supporting or condoning . . . homosexual activity or bisexual activity." In 2015 Lutheran High North forced seventeen-year-old Austin Wallis to leave school because he had come out as gay on his YouTube video blog. The principal had given Wallis the choice of staying if he deleted his online videos and hid his sexual orientation, which Wallis felt he could not do. "This YouTube channel means the world to me," he said in a video. "I love feeling like this helps people. It means a lot to me that I might help a few people that might be feeling like they're not worth it."[41] The school's administration claimed that Wallis's videos promoted homosexuality and reflected poorly on the school—even though Wallis stated in his videos that he planned on waiting until marriage to be sexually active. Private schools like Lutheran High North can legally deny enrollment to students for being LGBT.

> " Suicide among LGBT youth has reached epidemic proportions. "

Homophobia and Suicide

It is impossible to know the exact suicide rate of LGBT teens because many of their deaths are not reported as being related to their sexual orientation or gender identity. However, many experts say that suicide among LGBT youth has reached epidemic proportions. In the first four months of 2015 at least seven transgender teens committed suicide in the United States. A 2011 study published in the journal *Pediatrics* found that 21.5 percent of LGBT youth had attempted suicide, compared to 4.2 percent of non-LGBT youth. And according to a 2011 survey by the Williams Institute, 41 percent of transgender people have attempted suicide.

Because teens are increasingly recording their experiences with homophobia on social media, their struggles are becoming more public. Sixteen-year-old Taylor Alesana, a transgender girl in Fallbrook, California, spoke out in a series of YouTube videos about the daily harassment she faced at school. "Being transgender, for me, [means] I've lost tons of friends—tons. It's been hell."[42] Even though she spoke out about trans issues in her videos and claimed that she did not care about the constant harassment at school, she ended her life over spring break in 2015.

Alesana was one of dozens of recent suicides by teens who spoke out about their struggles online before taking their lives. These teens are reaching out to their communities and receiving support, yet it is still not enough to counteract the effects of homophobia and harassment—problems that transwoman Greta Martela, director of Trans Lifeline, describes as "chronic, long-lasting, and generally beyond the power of the individual to remedy." As Martela explains, "The problems faced by transgender people don't need to be solved by transgender people alone. It's up to everyone else."[43]

Primary Source Quotes*

What Challenges Do LGBT Teens Face?

❝My high school is extremely good with the LGBTQ+ stuff. . . . Most everyone is perfectly fine with your sexuality/ gender identity, and there are signs everywhere that say, 'This is a safe space for LGBTQ+ individuals.'❞

—Iswearimpopular, "Life: What's It Like at Your School?," forum post, JustLefttheCloset.com, January 3, 2015. www.justleftthecloset.com.

Iswearimpopular is the screen name of a female teen who identifies as non-binary (not exclusively male or female), demisexual (only sexually attracted if emotionally connected), and panromantic (romantically attracted to any gender). She attends high school in the United States.

❝We don't have LGBT support groups [at school]. . . . Even if you simply wish to take a same-sexed partner to . . . [prom], your parents need to sign permission slips and you're forced to go to compulsory counseling, as though you have a problem.❞

—Likewatercolors, "Life: What's It Like at Your School?," forum post, JustLefttheCloset.com, March 14, 2012. www.justleftthecloset.com.

Likewatercolors is the screen name of a lesbian teen who attends a Catholic high school in Australia. She says that many of the teachers and students are homophobic, and it is not safe to come out as LGBT.

Bracketed quotes indicate conflicting positions.

* Editor's Note: While the definition of a primary source can be narrowly or broadly defined, for the purposes of Compact Research, a primary source consists of: 1) results of original research presented by an organization or researcher; 2) eyewitness accounts of events, personal experience, or work experience; 3) first-person editorials offering pundits' opinions; 4) government officials presenting political plans and/or policies; 5) representatives of organizations presenting testimony or policy.

“The idea of having an LGBT child is no longer a horrifying possibility for many parents, and many educated young parents in particular would not dream of shaming their male child for liking dresses or their girl for refusing to wear them.”

—Margaret Nichols, “LGBT Youth Suicide: As Serious as It Is Preventable,” GoodTherapy.org, September 16, 2013. www.goodtherapy.org.

Nichols is a psychologist and executive director of the Institute for Personal Growth, a psychotherapy practice that has special expertise in working with LGBT issues.

“For a kid who got bullied, beat up and nearly killed for once trying to kiss a girl in high school, I am doing all right now.”

—Margaret Cho, Twitter, May 12, 2013. https://twitter.com.

Cho is a Korean American comedian and actor who identifies as queer.

“Bullying almost always has a homophobic component to it. It seems that the greatest insult you can hurl at a kid is calling him gay.”

—GLBT National Help Center Blog, “School Bullying + Easy Guns + Mental Illness = School Violence,” November 17, 2013. https://glbtnhc.wordpress.com.

The GLBT National Help Center provides free and confidential peer support to GLBTQ people.

“It takes a special kind of awareness to live in the world as a queer person. It takes great strength to have one’s sexual identity invested with so much meaning by strangers.”

—W. Blue, “Happy National Coming Out Day,” *Psychology Today*, October 11, 2014. www.psychologytoday.com.

Blue is a freelance writer from Brooklyn, New York, who writes about queer issues.

❝For people who do not fit the conventional sex and gender roles, it is hard to find role models and equally difficult to find acceptance from family, peers, and society.❞

—Julia Wood, *Gendered Lives: Communication, Gender, & Culture.* Stamford, CT: Cengage Learning, 2015, p. 161.

Wood, a professor of communication studies at the University of North Carolina, researches the intersections of gender, communication, and culture.

❝I've definitely gotten some . . . really weird looks in the women's restroom . . . and in the men's restroom as well, although I just don't feel safe in the men's restroom.❞

—Scott Morrison, interview by Hillary Wittier of WPIX New York, "Oregon's Grant High School Creates Gender-Neutral Restrooms for Transgender Students," *Huffington Post*, March 25, 2015. www.huffingtonpost.com.

Morrison is a transgender boy at Ulysses S. Grant High School in Portland, Oregon. The high school recently designated several single stall bathrooms as unisex.

Facts and Illustrations

What Challenges Do LGBT Teens Face?

- In 2011 a study published in the journal *Pediatrics* found that **21.5 percent** of LGBT youth had attempted suicide, compared to **4.2 percent** of non-LGBT youth.

- According to a 2011 survey by the Williams Institute, **41 percent** of transgender people have attempted suicide.

- According to psychologist Margaret Nichols, **85 to 90 percent of LGBT youth** are verbally harassed at school, **40 percent** are physically harassed, and **20 percent** are physically assaulted.

- According to the website bullyingstatistics.org, of LGBT students who miss school because of bullying, **28 percent** feel forced to drop out of school altogether.

- According to the Forty to None Project, even though LGBT youth represent about **3 to 5 percent** of the total youth population, they make up **20 to 40 percent** of all homeless young people.

- According to the National LGBTQ Task Force's Policy Institute, **50 percent** of gay male teens experienced a negative reaction from their parents when they came out, and **26 percent** were kicked out of their homes.

- In a 2012 survey of LGBT teens by the Human Rights Campaign, only **37 percent** describe themselves as happy, as compared to **67 percent** of straight teens.

Most LGBT Students Avoid School Activities

Involvement in extracurricular clubs or special events can increase teens' self-esteem, academic achievement, and sense of belonging at school. However, a study published in 2014 found that many LGBT students avoid these activities frequently, often, or sometimes because they feel unsafe or uncomfortable. The study's authors note that this may indicate that LGBT students are being discouraged from participating in these activities.

Percentage of LGBT Students Who Said They Avoid School Activities Because They Feel Uncomfortable or Unsafe

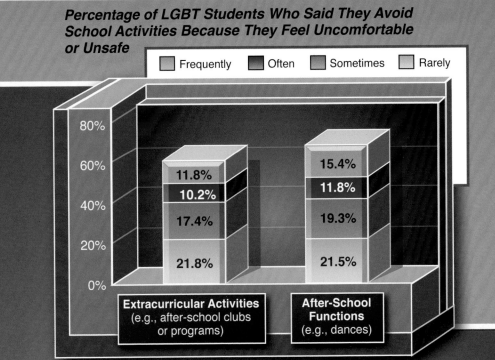

Legend: Frequently | Often | Sometimes | Rarely

Extracurricular Activities (e.g., after-school clubs or programs):
- 11.8%
- 10.2%
- 17.4%
- 21.8%

After-School Functions (e.g., dances):
- 15.4%
- 11.8%
- 19.3%
- 21.5%

Source: Joseph Kosciw, et al., *The 2013 National School Climate Survey.* GLSEN, 2014, p.13. www.slj.com.

- According to the Family Acceptance Project, gay and transgender teens who are highly rejected by their parents and caregivers are more than eight times as likely to have attempted suicide, nearly six times as likely to report high levels of depression, and more than three times as likely to use illegal drugs and to be at high risk for HIV and sexually transmitted diseases.

Why LGBT Youth Are Homeless

A survey by the Williams Institute found that 40 percent of homeless youth in America are LGBT, and 89 percent of these youth were forced to leave their homes or ran away because their families rejected their sexual orientation or gender identity. The report surveyed more than 350 homeless service providers around the country. Only one-quarter of these programs are specifically designed for LGBT clients.

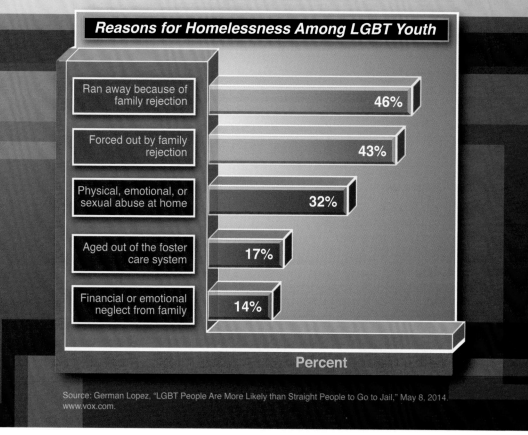

Reasons for Homelessness Among LGBT Youth

Reason	Percent
Ran away because of family rejection	46%
Forced out by family rejection	43%
Physical, emotional, or sexual abuse at home	32%
Aged out of the foster care system	17%
Financial or emotional neglect from family	14%

Percent

Source: German Lopez, "LGBT People Are More Likely than Straight People to Go to Jail," May 8, 2014. www.vox.com.

- The Human Rights Campaign survey also found that only **5 percent** of transgender youth reported "definitely fitting in" in their community.

- A 2013 GLSEN national survey of LGBT youth found that over one-third avoid gender-segregated spaces like bathrooms and locker rooms because they feel unsafe or uncomfortable.

Most LGBT Adults Have Experienced Discrimination

A 2013 online survey of almost two thousand LGBT adults found that most had experienced discrimination or victimization because of their sexual orientation or gender identity. Most instances of discrimination, survey participants said, had occurred earlier in their lives.

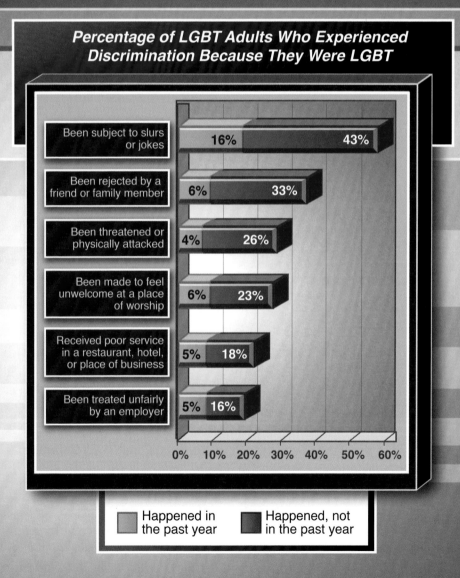

Percentage of LGBT Adults Who Experienced Discrimination Because They Were LGBT

Category	Happened in the past year	Happened, not in the past year
Been subject to slurs or jokes	16%	43%
Been rejected by a friend or family member	6%	33%
Been threatened or physically attacked	4%	26%
Been made to feel unwelcome at a place of worship	6%	23%
Received poor service in a restaurant, hotel, or place of business	5%	18%
Been treated unfairly by an employer	5%	16%

Source: Pew Research Center, "A Survey of LGBT Americans," June 13, 2013. www.pewsocialtrends.org.

How Can Teens Get Help with LGBT Issues?

66I wanted to show America a different kind of man. If there was someone like me when I was growing up, my whole life would have been different.99

—Dancing with the Stars contestant Chaz Bono, a transgender man who was criticized for appearing on a family-friendly television show.

66Remember, the change you want to see in the world, and in your school, begins with you.99

—Joseph Clementi, whose eighteen-year-old gay son, Tyler, committed suicide after being bullied by his college roommate. The Clementi family founded the Tyler Clementi Foundation to raise awareness of bullying and cyberbullying against LGBT youth.

One of the keys to dealing with LGBT issues is to have a strong support system. Having friends, allies, and trusted adults to talk to can help LGBT teens deal with problems such as homophobia, discrimination, and depression. They can also help teens forge an LGBT identity and give them confidence to tackle the issues that matter to them head-on.

LGBT Friends

Having friends who are LGBT makes a huge difference in the life of an LGBT teen. As Kathy Belge and Marke Bieschke explain in the book *Queer: The Ultimate LGBT Guide for Teens*, "It can be such a relief to finally find others who get your sense of style, who know what it's like to be different, and who you can talk to about anything without being judged or feeling out of place."[44] However, this community may be hard to find. While some teens are lucky enough to go to a school with an active LGBT community of students, others can feel isolated, believing that they are the only one in their school or their neighborhood who is LGBT.

> "Having friends who are LGBT makes a huge difference in the life of an LGBT teen.

A good place to start is looking online for a listing of LGBT social organizations in the community. The Trevor Project, a crisis intervention group for LGBTQ teens and young adults, contains a searchable database of local LGBT resources, including teen social organizations. National support and education groups such as PFLAG (Parents, Families, and Friends of Lesbians and Gays) often facilitate social groups for teens. Public librarians are often knowledgeable about how to find local support groups and can help with Internet searches. In lieu of local organizations, there are vibrant communities online where LGBT teens can seek support and make friends. Forums like www.emptyclosets.com and www.justleftthecloset.com allow teens to meet other LGBT teens, exchange information, and support each other.

Having people to talk with face-to-face allows LGBT teens to develop deep friendships that are not possible online. However, LGBT people are all so different from one another that teens may find it hard to find anyone like them. Bieschke suggests that teens give other LGBT teens a chance, even if they seem different. When Bieschke first came out, it did not seem like he had anything in common with the other gay people in his school. "I took a giant social leap and befriended the gayest-acting guy in school," he remembers. Even though they liked very different things, he became Bieschke's best friend. "I met an entire network of other queer kids through [my friend]. . . . Finally, I could relax and be myself around other LGBT people."[45]

Allies and Trusted Adults

Another key to an LGBT teen's support system is having trusted adults to reach out to for help and advice. Those adults do not have to be LGBT, but if they are, they may be better able to relate to the unique issues that face LGBT teens. They can also offer useful advice about dealing with discrimination from adults and may be able to advise teens about their legal rights.

Teachers often become allies for LGBT teens. To determine whether a teacher is supportive, teens can take note of whether the teacher reprimands homophobic remarks in his or her classroom (such as use of the saying "that's so gay"). Adults at local LGBT support centers such as PFLAG also tend to be extremely understanding as well as have specialized knowledge and a network of resources to turn to for help.

Creating an LGBT Identity

Straight and cisgender people do not usually think of their sexual orientation or their gender as the core part of their identity. However, many LGBT people find that having to struggle against heterosexual and cisgender norms—for equal rights, or for respect, or for acceptance—makes the LGBT part of them much more central to their identity.

If it is true that the best defense is a good offense, then deliberately forging an LGBT identity is one of the best ways to fight back against the often debilitating effects of homophobia and discrimination. Teens who know who they are and what they stand for tend to be far less afraid to speak out against discrimination and hate and to stand up for their rights. They also are more likely to develop confidence and an inner strength that can see them through difficult times.

> " **Key to an LGBT teen's support system is having trusted adults to reach out to for help and advice.** "

An excellent way for teens to figure out their identities is through their LGBT peers, friends, and adult allies. By discussing issues and sharing experiences, teens learn what matters to them. Some teens join their local LGBT organization and help out with community building activities or education outreach to the community. Others are interested in fighting for equal rights, and may decide to support a political candidate who wants to end discrimination against LGBT people. Many teens reach out to other teens on the Internet by starting a video blog or website, such as Austin Wallis did when he first came out as gay. When he was forced to leave his religious high school, his blog became a platform to reach out to other teens who had also experienced discrimination.

Fighting School Discrimination

Many public schools believe they have the right to discriminate against LGBT students because, they claim, LGBT activities are disruptive or reflect poorly on the school as a whole. Other schools apply their own policies unfairly, enforcing rules on LGBT students only. For instance, a common complaint among LGB students is that school administrations often discipline same-sex public displays of affection, like holding hands or kissing in the halls, while ignoring opposite sex behaviors. According to the American Civil Liberties Union (ACLU), federal laws require that public schools apply policy rules fairly across the entire student body. For instance, the federal Equal Access Act says that administrations are not allowed to stop students from forming a GSA if they allow other noncurricular clubs, such as Chess Club.

> By discussing issues and sharing experiences, teens learn what matters to them.

Public schools also have the same responsibilities to protect LGBT students from harassment and bullying as they have toward straight and cisgender students. According to the ACLU, trans students have special protection under Title IX, the Equal Opportunity in Education Act, which prohibits sex-based discrimination in public schools. The ACLU states:

Title IX bars public schools from ignoring harassment based on gender stereotyping. . . . They can't ignore harassment based on appearance or behavior that doesn't "match" your gender: boys who wear makeup, girls who dress "like a boy," or students who are transgender. Nor can school officials tell you that you have to change who you are or that the harassment is your fault because of how you dress and act.[46]

The law is complicated, and sometimes it is necessary to bring a lawsuit against a school to force it to end discriminatory practices. In 2015 the Justice Department under the Obama Administration supported one of these lawsuits brought by a transgender boy, who is suing several schools for failing to protect him from bullying and revealing confidential information about him to other parents. "The rights that are being violated are important United States constitutional rights,"[47] said the youth's attorney, James Rasor.

School Activism

Sometimes the most effective way to fight discrimination and harassment at school is to educate the administration and other students about LGBT issues. Teens who are looking for a way to make things better for the LGBT community often need to go no farther than their own school.

Unfortunately, it can take a tragedy like the suicide of an LGBT teen for a school administration to realize that a change is necessary. According-ing to psychologist Margaret Nichols, change starts with the attitude of the administration. "We have seen schools where administrators, teachers, parents, and students alike embraced these [trans] kids and made them feel safe and cared about," says Nichols. "And we have seen trans kids literally made suicidal by the callous, cruel, ignorant culture of other schools."[48]

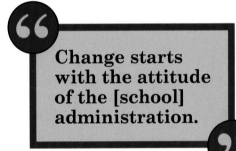

Change starts with the attitude of the [school] administration.

Several organizations have educational programs for school faculty and students alike. One of them is GLSEN's Safe Space Campaign. Historically, a safe space is a place where people can feel free to express their points of view and be themselves without fear of being mocked or belittled. The Safe Space Campaign has training materials designed for school faculty on how to educate students about anti-LGBT bias and support students who are LGBT. They also suggest ways that concerned students and adults can change policy at their school. Teachers can post safe space stickers and posters declaring classrooms to be "a safe and in-clusive space"[49] for LGBT students.

Educating Through GSAs

Studies have shown that one of the best ways to raise awareness among straight and cisgender students about LGBT issues is to form a GSA. GSAs work to bring straight and LGBT students together to support each other. They often organize events to fight homophobia and transphobia. Teens seeking to make changes in their schools often start by forming a GSA. It is much easier to approach a school administration about making policy changes as a GSA than as a lone student. National GSA support groups such as the National Association of GSA Networks can help teens form GSAs in their schools.

> " **Bullied LGBT teens sometimes feel as though they are somehow to blame for the harassment.** "

Many GSAs organize annual events that support LGBT students. One such event is National Coming Out Day, which occurs on October 11, the anniversary of the National March on Washington, DC, for Lesbian and Gay Rights in 1987. The Day of Silence, created by GLSEN to spread awareness about the effects of bullying and harassment on LGBT students, is held in April. According to the website www.dayof silence.org, "Students from middle school to college take a vow of silence in an effort to encourage schools and classmates to address the problem of anti-LGBT behavior by illustrating the silencing effect of bullying and harassment on LGBT students and those perceived to be LGBT."[50]

Dealing with Bullying and Harassment

Many LGBT students who experience bullying and harassment do not report the bullying to the administration. Sometimes they are afraid that they will make the harassment worse or that it is not safe for them to do so. Teens caught in this situation need support—from friends, trusted adults, or counselors. In-person friendships with other LGBT teens can be an effective way to limit the devastating effect of bullying and harassment. Talking the situation over with a trusted adult can also help, as can researching what other students have done to find relief.

Teens who feel as though there is no way to stop harassment at school often become depressed. Depression is a serious illness that can cause sufferers to blame themselves for their predicament. This means that bullied LGBT teens sometimes feel as though they are somehow to blame for the harassment they face. Teens who feel this way are at risk of self-harm—whether that is in the form of alcohol and drug abuse, behaviors like cutting, or suicide. It is important that they seek out an LGBT-supportive health care professional, such as a therapist or psychiatrist, as soon as possible to help them with their depressive symptoms.

The It Gets Better Project

In 2010, in response to a spate of suicides of teenagers who were bullied because they were LGBT, gay activist and journalist Dan Savage created the It Gets Better Project. The project encourages adults to submit videos that assure LGBT teens that bullying and harassment eventually end, and life improves. More than fifty thousand user-created videos have been submitted, including messages from President Barack Obama and Secretary of State Hillary Clinton. In 2012 Savage also published a collection of essays entitled *It Gets Better: Coming Out, Overcoming Bullying, and Creating a Life Worth Living.*

Since the project started in 2010, research has confirmed that life really does get better for LGBT teens. A study by Northwestern University found that as LGBT teens became adults, their levels of reported psychological distress and victimization both dropped steadily. "I think we should be very happy that it does get better, but I think it's important not to forget victimization is important and happens very early," says Michelle Birkett, the study's lead author. "It's not good enough to just wait. It should be tackled early on so kids don't have to experience it."[51]

Primary Source Quotes*

How Can Teens Get Help
with LGBT Issues?

> **If I can start early on and put [a transgender child] through the puberty that matches their gender identity, they're going to assimilate better.**

—Johanna Olson, "Early vs. Later Intervention for Gender Non-Conforming Children," video clip, Kidsinthehouse.com, May 17, 2013. www.kidsinthehouse.com.

Olson is the medical director of the Center for Transyouth Health and Development at Children's Hospital in Los Angeles, California.

> **[Prescribing] hormone-suppressing drugs to prevent preteens from going through puberty the better to prepare them for 'gender reassignment' surgery . . . is child abuse.**

—Mona Charen, "Our Crazed Sexuality Standards," *National Review*, January 14, 2014. www.nationalreview.com.

Charen is a senior fellow at the Ethics and Public Policy Institute in Washington, DC, a politically conservative advocacy group.

Bracketed quotes indicate conflicting positions.

* Editor's Note: While the definition of a primary source can be narrowly or broadly defined, for the purposes of Compact Research, a primary source consists of: 1) results of original research presented by an organization or researcher; 2) eyewitness accounts of events, personal experience, or work experience; 3) first-person editorials offering pundits' opinions; 4) government officials presenting political plans and/or policies; 5) representatives of organizations presenting testimony or policy.

66 **Effective social support can . . . [reduce] the negative impact of bullying [on LGBT teens].** 99

—Center for Mental Health in Schools, "Bullying and LGBT Students," University of California at Los Angeles, March 16, 2014. http://smhp.psych.ucla.edu.

The Center for Mental Health in Schools aims to enhance the field of mental health in schools to improve outcomes for young people.

66 **While any social support the young people received while being bullied tended to reduce their chances of depression, this benefit was usually short-lived.** 99

—Benjamin Ryan, "It Really Might 'Get Better' for LGBT Teens," *Atlantic*, February 13, 2015. www.theatlantic.com.

Ryan is the editor at large for *POZ*, a magazine for people living with and affected by HIV/AIDS.

66 **If you can ask yourself, 'Am I being true to who I am? Am I happy with what I look like, with the way I dress, how I act. Am I being true to me?' If the answer is yes, then it is possible to still be a happy and well adjusted person even in a world that doesn't always understand you.** 99

—Ashley Wylde, "Is That a Girl or a Boy?," YouTube, April 21, 2014. https://www.youtube.com/watch?v=WN1wWf_eJ34.

Wylde is a spoken word poet and entertainer. She identifies as a woman but is often mistaken for a man.

66 **Imagine the impact that an openly gay athlete would have on a growing-but-struggling LGBT teen boy. The message that boy would get would be, 'You're fine just the way you are, you can do whatever it is in life you want to do, and I'm proof that it truly will get better.' That's potentially life-saving.** 99

—Ron Kemp, "The Importance of Gay Role Models," *Enough Is Enough*, blog, June 8, 2012. http://ronkemp.blogspot.com.

Kemp is a gay man who writes about gay teen suicide on his blog *Enough Is Enough*.

❝LGBT young people whose parents and caregivers . . . support them show greater well-being, better general health, and significantly decreased risk for suicide, depression, and substance abuse.❞

—Caitlin Ryan, *A Practitioner's Resource Guide: Helping Families to Support Their LGBT Children*, HHS Publication No. PEP14-LGBTKIDS. Rockville, MD: Substance Abuse and Mental Health Services Administration, 2014. http://familyproject.sfsu.edu.

Ryan is the director and cofounder of the Family Acceptance Project at San Francisco State University, which assists families in supporting LGBT youth.

❝Without my GSA, I wouldn't have had the chance to achieve a feat like becoming an FTM [female to male] homecoming king.❞

—Mel Gonzales, "From Heartbreak to Homecoming: How I Transformed My School for LGBTQ Youth," GSA Network, November 3, 2014. www.gsanetwork.org.

Gonzales, who started a GSA at his high school, later became the first trans homecoming king in Texas.

How Can Teens Get Help with LGBT Issues?

- A 2014 Canadian study found that when schools had gay-straight alliances and policies in place for three or more years, LGB students had fewer suicidal thoughts and attempts.

- According to the CDC, research has established that LGBT students in schools that have LGBT support groups are less likely to experience threats of violence or miss school because they feel unsafe than LGBT students in schools without support groups.

- According to a survey of **5,542 teens** published in 2015 in *Psychology Today*, **62 percent** of gay, lesbian, or queer youth are likely to make friends online, as compared to **25 percent** of cisgender heterosexual youth.

- GLSEN reports in its 2013 National School Climate Survey that students in schools with GSAs are less likely to hear homophobic remarks in school on a daily basis (**57 percent**) compared to students without GSAs (**75 percent**).

- GLSEN also reports that **24 percent** of students in schools with GSAs say they hear teachers make supportive or positive remarks about lesbian and gay people, as compared to **12 percent** of students in schools without such clubs.

When Bullying Decreases, Psychological Distress Decreases

A study published in 2015 found that one reason why psychological distress such as depression and anxiety decreases as LGBT teens get older may be because bullying and other victimization decreases as well. The study examined the experiences of 231 LGBTQ adolescents aged sixteen to twenty over a 3.5-year period. It found that psychological distress was related to victimization and that, on average, both decreased between the ages of sixteen to twenty-four.

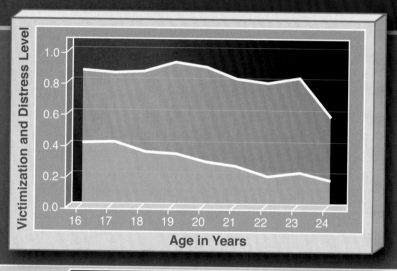

Variables

Mean Victimization, past 6 months

Mean Psychological Distress

Source: M. Birkett, ME Newcomb, and B. Mustanki, "Does It Get Better? A Longitudinal Analysis of Psychological Distress and Victimization in Lesbian, Gay, Bisexual, Transgender, and Questioning Youth," *Journal of Adolescent Health*, March 2015, p. 283.

- As of May 4, 2015, **598,552 people** had taken the It Gets Better pledge and vowed to speak up against hate and intolerance.

- In 2010 teenager Brittany McMillan started Spirit Day, in which supporters of LGBT teens wear purple as a stand against bullying.

Gay-Straight Alliances Promote Respectful Environments

A study published in 2014 found that students who attend schools that have gay-straight alliance clubs (GSAs) are less likely to make anti-LGBT remarks. The national online survey of LGBT students in grades six through twelve found that, in schools without a GSA, nearly three-quarters of LGBT students heard homophobic remarks like "fag" or "dyke" often or frequently, as compared to only 57.4 percent of students in schools with a GSA. The study's authors concluded that GSAs can help create a more inclusive and respectful school environment for LGBT students.

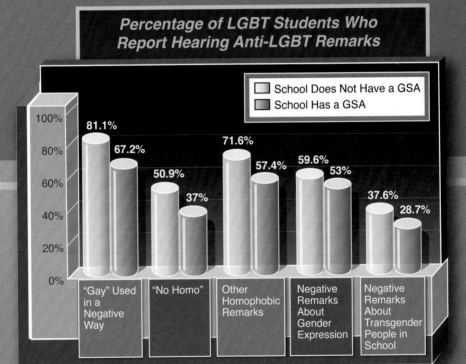

Percentage of LGBT Students Who Report Hearing Anti-LGBT Remarks

Source: Joseph Kosciw et al., *The 2013 National School Climate Survey.* GLSEN, 2014, p. 66. www.slj.com.

- According to the *Princeton Review*, the most LGBT-friendly college in the United States is New York University.

LGBT Youth Use the Internet for Information and Support

The Internet is an important source of information and support for LGBT youth. A study published in the *Journal of Sex Research* examined the Internet habits of thirty-two LGBT youth ages sixteen to twenty-four. More than half used the Internet to meet other LGBT youth, and more than a third used it to better understand their identities or to find out about LGBT events or services. The authors note that using the Internet in these ways often increased the participants' confidence and self-esteem, especially in those who had few offline resources.

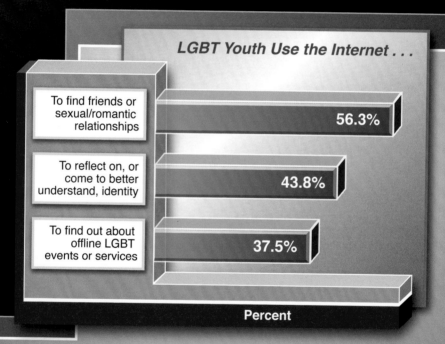

LGBT Youth Use the Internet . . .

To find friends or sexual/romantic relationships	56.3%
To reflect on, or come to better understand, identity	43.8%
To find out about offline LGBT events or services	37.5%

Percent

Source: Samantha DeHann, et al., "The Interplay Between Online and Offline Explorations of Identity, Relationships, and Sex: A Mixed-Methods Study with LGBT Youth," *The Journal of Sex Research*, 2013, pp. 421–34.

- A 2011 study by the FAP found that students whose schools had a GSA were more likely to have higher self-esteem and less likely to experience depression.

- The FAP study also found that students at a school with a GSA were less likely to drop out and more likely to succeed in college.

- Inspired by the popular young adult novel *The Misfits*, GLSEN created No Name Calling week in 2004 to encourage schools to eliminate bullying.

- According to the GSA Network, an organization that helps LGBT students set up GSAs in their schools, **35 states** have a GSA network in place.

Key People and Advocacy Groups

American Institute of Bisexuality: A foundation that promotes and funds research and education about bisexuality.

Chaz Bono: An American writer, musician, and LGBT advocate, Bono is a transgender man. He was also the first openly transman to star in a major network television show (*Dancing with the Stars*) in a function unrelated to being transgender.

Barney Frank: The first US Representative to voluntarily come out as gay, Frank served in Congress from 1980 to 2013.

Lady Gaga: An award-winning American singer, songwriter, and performer who champions LGBT social movements and same-sex marriage. Gaga established the Born This Way Foundation, which focuses on youth empowerment.

Gay Lesbian Alliance Against Defamation (GLAAD): A multimedia watchdog organization dedicated to promoting fair, accurate, and inclusive representation of LGBTQ individuals in the media.

Human Rights Campaign (HRC): The largest national LGBTQ advocacy organization in the United States, HRC lobbies Congress and works to educate the public on equality issues.

Caitlyn Jenner: In an April 2015 interview with Diane Sawyer on the ABC television news magazine 20/20, former Olympic gold medalist Bruce Jenner publicly revealed that he was in the process of transforming into Caitlyn Jenner. Jenner told Sawyer that he had struggled throughout his life with gender identity. Caitlyn Jenner appeared on the cover of the July 2015 issue of *Vanity Fair* magazine; the photo and article revealed to the world her new identity.

Kevin Jennings: The founder of the first GSA, Jennings later became the executive director of the Gay, Lesbian & Straight Education Network (GLSEN).

Cyndi Lauper: An American singer, songwriter, actor, and LGBT activist, Lauper founded the Forty to None project to end LGBT teen homelessness.

Harvey Milk: A gay activist, politician, and symbol for gay rights, Milk was assassinated in 1978.

National LGBTQ Task Force: An advocacy group that seeks to advance freedom, justice, and equality for LGBTQ people through activism and its annual conference, the National Conference on LGBT Equality: Creating Change.

President Barack Obama: The first US president to support gay marriage, Obama ended the ban on LGBT persons serving in the military, made health care more accessible to LGBT persons, and worked to prevent LGBT bullying in schools.

Out and Equal Workplace Advocates: An advocacy organization that supports a safe and equitable workplace for LGBT people.

Geena Rocero: Transgender model and advocate, Rocero is founder of Gender Proud, an advocacy and aid organization that serves transgender people worldwide.

Dan Savage: A journalist, author, and gay activist who created the It Gets Better Project, which asks adults to submit video messages to LGBT youth encouraging them about the future.

Sexual Minority Youth Assistance League (SMYAL): An advocacy group that supports and empowers LGBT youth by creating opportunities for service and LGBT advocacy.

Chronology

1973
Homosexuality is no longer considered to be a mental illness and is removed from the *Diagnostic and Statistical Manual* of the American Psychological Association.

1996
Congress passes the Defense of Marriage Act, which defines marriage as the union of a man and a woman and allows states to refuse to recognize same sex marriages from other states.

1988
The first GSA is formed by Kevin Jennings in Concord, Massachusetts, at Concord Academy, a private high school.

1970

1990

2000

2004
Massachusetts is the first state to legalize same-sex marriage.

1991
The first GSA at a public high school is formed in Newton, Massachusetts, at South Newton High School.

1987
The National March on Washington for Lesbian and Gay Rights—often referred to as "The Great March" by gay historians—occurs on October 11.

1998
The GSA Network is formed as a way to bring together forty GSAs in the San Francisco Bay area so that they can share resources and interact with each other.

2010
Journalist and gay activist Dan Savage creates the It Gets Better Project in response to a rash of LGBT suicides among teens and young people, including eighteen-year-old Tyler Clementi.

2015
Gender-neutral restrooms are added to the White House.

2012
California becomes the first state to ban performing conversion therapy on minors.

2010

2015

2011
Rebecca Arellano and Haileigh Adams become the first gay royals in homecoming history at Patrick Henry High School in San Diego.

2013
The Defense of Marriage Act is found to be unconstitutional by the US Supreme Court and is repealed.

2009
Congress passes the Matthew Shepard Act, which outlaws hate crimes based on both sexual orientation and gender identity. Shepard was a twenty-one-year-old gay student who was beaten to death.

2014
Facebook adds more than fifty customizable gender options for users who do not identify as male or female.

Related Organizations

Bisexual Resource Center
PO Box 170796
Boston, MA 02116
e-mail: info@biresource.net • website: www.biresource.net

The Bisexual Resource Center provides support to the bisexual community, advocates for bisexual visibility, and raises awareness about bisexuality. Its website contains information about bisexuality, resources, news, and an educational section for youth.

Family Acceptance Project (FAP)
San Francisco State University
1600 Holloway Ave.
San Francisco, CA 94132
phone: (415) 522-5558
e-mail: fap@sfsu.edu • website: http://familyproject.sfsu.edu

FAP is a national research, education, and training institute that helps families to support their LGBT children. Its website includes reports on LGBT teen homelessness as well as a list of resources.

Gay, Lesbian & Straight Education Network (GLSEN)
90 Broad St., 2nd Floor
New York, NY 10004
phone: (212) 727-0135
e-mail: info@glsen.org • website: http://glsen.org

GLSEN's mission is to end LGBTQ discrimination, harassment, and bullying in schools. Its website contains national reports and briefs including the National School Climate Survey, articles, book chapters, webinars, and other educational materials.

GLBT National Help Center
2261 Market St., #296
San Francisco, CA 94114
phone: (415) 355-0003
GLBT youth talkline: 1 (800) 246-7743

e-mail: help@GLBThotline.org • website: www.glbthotline.org

GLBT National Help Center provides free and confidential peer support to LGBT teens and adults. Peer counselors can give information via phone or online chat about relationships, bullying, safer sex, resources, coming out, and other LGBT issues. Its website contains FAQs, resources, and a blog.

The GSA Network

1550 Bryant St., Suite 600
San Francisco, CA 94103
phone: (415) 552-4229 • fax: (415) 552-4729
e-mail: info@gsanetwork.org • website: www.gsanetwork.org

The GSA Network coordinates more than nine hundred GSAs in the United States. It trains queer, trans, and allied youth leaders to advocate, organize, and mobilize GSAs to create safer schools and healthier communities. Its website has information about forming and running a GSA, news, and a blog.

Lambda Legal

120 Wall St., 19th Floor
New York, NY 10005-3919
phone: (212) 809-8585 • fax: (212) 809-0055
website: www.lambdalegal.org

Lambda Legal is the oldest and largest national legal organization whose mission is to achieve full recognition of the civil rights of lesbians, gay men, bisexuals, transgender people, and those with HIV through impact litigation, education, and public policy work. Its website contains information about the legal rights of LGBT persons, as well as publications, resources, and a blog about LGBT rights.

National Center for Transgender Equality

1325 Massachusetts Ave. NW, Suite 700
Washington, DC 20005
phone: (202) 903-0112 • fax: (202) 393-2241
e-mail: ncte@transequality.org • website: http://transequality.org

The National Center for Transgender Equality is a social justice organization devoted to ending discrimination and violence against transgender people through education and advocacy on issues of importance to transgender people. Its website contains information about issues pertaining to transgender persons, resources about transgender rights under the law, and a blog.

National Federation of Parents and Friends of Lesbians and Gays (PFLAG)

1828 L St. NW, Suite 660
Washington, DC 20036
phone: (202) 467-8180 • fax: (202) 467-8194
e-mail: info@pflag.org • website: www.pflag.org

PFLAG is a national organization for education, advocacy, and support for families and friends of LGBT persons. PFLAG's website has information and news about LGBT issues and supporting LGBT persons and their families.

The Trevor Project

PO Box 69232
West Hollywood, CA 90069
phone: (310) 271-8845
Trevor suicide prevention hotline: (866) 488-7386
e-mail: info@thetrevorproject.org • website: www.thetrevorproject.org

The Trevor Project provides crisis intervention and suicide prevention services to LGBTQ youth by phone or chat. Its website has a social networking site, a support center, a blog, and a wealth of resources and information about LGBTQ issues.

Youth Resource

Advocates for Youth
2000 M St. NW, Suite 750
Washington, DC 20036
phone: (202) 419-3420 • fax: (202) 419-1448
e-mail: information@advocatesforyouth.org
website: www.youthresource.com

Youth Resource is an online resource created by and for LGBTQ young people. Members can access message boards, online peer education, and monthly features. Membership is free. Its website contains information about LGBT issues and health topics, as well as crisis hotlines.

For Further Research

Books

Michael Bronski, Ann Pellegrini, and Michael Amico, *"You Can Tell Just By Looking": And 20 Other Myths About LGBT Life and People*. Boston: Beacon, 2013.

Jason Cianciotto and Sean Cahill, *LGBT Youth in America's Schools*. Ann Arbor, MI: University of Michigan Press, 2012.

Julie Sondra Decker, *The Invisible Orientation: An Introduction to Asexuality*. New York: Carrel, 2014.

Shiri Eisner, *Bi: Notes for a Bisexual Revolution*. Berkeley, CA: Seal, 2013.

Laura Erickson-Schroth, ed., *Trans Bodies, Trans Selves: A Resource for the Transgender Community*. New York: Oxford University Press, 2014.

Dan Savage, *American Savage: Insights, Slights, and Fights on Faith, Sex, Love, and Politics*. New York: Penguin Group, 2013.

Nicholas Teich, *Transgender 101: A Simple Guide to a Complex Issue*. New York: Columbia University Press, 2012.

Periodicals

W. Blue, "When Did You Know You Were Gay?," *Psychology Today*, July 15, 2014. www.psychologytoday.com/blog/queer-studies/201407/when-did-you-know-you-were-gay.

Dean Burnett, "Why Would People 'Choose' to Be Gay?," *Guardian*, January 8, 2015. www.theguardian.com/science/brain-flapping/2015/jan/08/homosexuality-gay-choice-psychology.

Julie Sondra Decker, "How to Tell If You Are Asexual," *Time*, June 18, 2014. http://time.com/2889469/asexual-orientation.

Benoit Denizet-Lewis, "The Scientific Quest to Prove Bisexuality Exists," *New York Times*, March 20, 2014. www.nytimes.com/2014/03/23/magazine/the-scientific-quest-to-prove-bisexuality-exists.html.

Sabrina Rubin Erdely, "One Town's War on Gay Teens," *Rolling Stone*,

February 2, 2013. www.rollingstone.com/politics/news/one-towns -war-on-gay-teens-20120202.

Jason Koebler, "Scientists May Have Finally Unlocked Puzzle of Why People Are Gay," *US News & World Report*, December 11, 2012. www.usnews.com/news/articles/2012/12/11/scientists-may-have -finally-unlocked-puzzle-of-why-people-are-gay.

Benjamin Ryan, "It Really Might 'Get Better' for LGBT Teens," *Atlantic*, February 13, 2015. www.theatlantic.com/health/archive/2015/02 /it-really-might-get-better-for-lgbt-teens/385467.

Michael Schulman, "Generation LGBTQIA," *New York Times*, January 9, 2013. www.nytimes.com/2013/01/10/fashion/generation-lgbtqia .html.

Margaret Talbot, "About a Boy," *New Yorker*, March 18, 2013. www .newyorker.com/magazine/2013/03/18/about-a-boy-2.

Rob Watson, "A Gay Dad Offers an Open Letter to the School That Rejected Out Teen," *Huffington Post*, February 23, 2015. www.huffing tonpost.com/2015/02/23/gay-dad-austlin-wallis-_n_6724378.html.

Internet Sources

Jillian Cottle, "Hallelujah, It's Raining Labels," *A Fine Line*, blog, July 16, 2011. http://jilliancottle.com/hallelujah-its-raining-labels.

Human Rights Campaign, "Growing Up LGBT in America," 2013. http://hrc-assets.s3-website-us-east-1.amazonaws.com//files/assets /resources/Growing-Up-LGBT-in-America_Report.pdf.

Human Rights Campaign, "The Lies and Dangers of Efforts to Change Sexual Orientation or Gender Identity." www.hrc.org/resources /entry/the-lies-and-dangers-of-reparative-therapy.

Joseph Kosciw et al., *The 2013 National School Climate Survey*, GLSEN, 2013. www.slj.com/wp-content/uploads/2014/10/2013-National-School-Climate-Survey-Full-Report.pdf.

Richard Reams, *'Am I Gay?' A Guide for People Who Question Their Sexual Orientation*, 2015. www.yoursexualorientation.info/Sexual_Orienta tion_Evidence.php.

Source Notes

Overview

1. The Trevor Project, "Glossary," 2015. www.thetrevorproject.org.
2. Kenneth Cohen and Ritch Savin-Williams, "Coming Out to Self and Others," in Petros Levounis, Jack Drescher, and Mary Barber, eds., *LGBT Casebook*. Arlington, VA: American Psychiatric Publishing, 2012, p. 18.
3. Quoted in Benoit Denizet-Lewis, "The Scientific Quest to Prove Bisexuality Exists," *New York Times*, March 20, 2014. www.nytimes.com.
4. Andrew Wagner, "Reclamation: Taking Back, Giving Away, and the Future of (Queer) Language," *Broad Recognition*, April 22, 2012. http://broadrecognition.com.
5. Jillian Cottle, "Hallelujah, It's Raining Labels," *A Fine Line*, blog, July 16, 2011. http://jilliancottle.com.
6. Natalie Reed, "Gender Expression Is Not Gender Identity," *Sincerely, Natalie Reed*, blog, March 21, 2012. http://freethoughtblogs.com.
7. Charice Pempengco, interview by Oprah Winfrey, *Charice's Coming-Out Story: "My Soul Is Male,"* video, Oprah Where Are They Now?, October 19, 2014. www.oprah.com.

How Do Teens Know If They Are LGBT?

8. Dean Burnett, "Why Would People 'Choose' to Be Gay?," *Guardian*, January 8, 2015. www.theguardian.com.
9. W. Blue, "When Did You Know You Were Gay?," *Psychology Today*, July 15, 2014. www.psychologytoday.com.
10. GLBT National Help Center, "Labels?," *GLBT National Help Center Blog*, May 29, 2013. https://glbtnhc.wordpress.com.
11. GLBT National Help Center, "Android's New 'Is My Son Gay?' App," *GLBT National Help Center Blog*, October 31, 2011. https://glbtnhc.wordpress.com.
12. Ashley Wylde, "Is That a Girl or a Boy?," YouTube, April 21, 2014. https://www.youtube.com/watch?v=WN1wWf_eJ34.
13. Ashley Wylde, "Everyday Gay FAQ," Tumblr. http://everydaygay.tumblr.com.
14. Quoted in Denizet-Lewis, "The Scientific Quest to Prove Bisexuality Exists."
15. Richard Reams, *'Am I Gay?' A Guide for People Who Question Their Sexual Orientation (Part 4)*, 2015. www.yoursexualorientation.info.
16. Reams, *'Am I Gay?' A Guide for People Who Question Their Sexual Orientation.*
17. Dara Hoffman-Fox, "How Do I Know If I'm Transgender?" YouTube, April 24, 2014. https://www.youtube.com/watch?v=Oea10Q5tG4Q.
18. Natasha Tracy, "Internalized Homophobia: Homophobia Within," HealthyPlace, January 14, 2014. www.healthyplace.com.
19. Quoted in Human Rights Campaign, "The Lies and Dangers of Efforts to Change Sexual Orientation or Gender Identity." www.hrc.org.
20. John Paul Brammer, "7 Things I Wish I Knew Before Coming Out as Gay," *Huffington Post*, November 16, 2014. www.huffingtonpost.com.

What Issues Do LGBT Teens Have with Coming Out?

21. AVERT, "Coming Out," 2014. www.avert.org.
22. W. Blue, "Coming Out," *Psychology Today*, July 29, 2014. www.psychologytoday.com.

23. Charlotte, "Charlotte," RUCO Stories, 2012. www.rucomingout.com.
24. Wayne Dhesi, "R U Coming Out?" www.rucomingout.com.
25. Montana, "Coming Out Story," JustLeftTheCloset.com. www.justleftthecloset.com.
26. Quoted in *Huffington Post*, "Caitlin Ryan's Story from the Let Love Define Family Series," October 3, 2014. www.huffingtonpost.com.
27. Quoted in Alexis Blue and Cathy Renna, "LGBT Teens Who Come Out at School Have Better Self-Esteem, Study Finds," UA News, February 9, 2015. http://uanews.org.
28. Jen, "Coming Out Story," JustLeftTheCloset.com. www.justleftthecloset.com.
29. Quoted in Crystal Proxmire, "Transgender Children Share Coming Out Stories," Pride Source, April 19, 2012. www.pridesource.com.
30. Planned Parenthood, "Coming Out at a Glance." www.plannedparenthood.org.

What Challenges Do LGBT Teens Face?

31. Human Rights Campaign, "Growing Up LGBT in America," 2013. http://hrc-assets.s3 website-us-east-1.amazonaws.com.
32. Merriam-Webster, online dictionary. www.merriam-webster.com.
33. Quoted in Louis Peitzman, "The New Documentary That Shows How Our Obsession with Masculinity Is Destroying Young Men," BuzzFeed, January 29, 2015. www.buzzfeed.com.
34. Michael Bronski, Ann Pellegrini, and Michael Amico, *"You Can Tell Just by Looking": And 20 Other Myths About LGBT Life and People.* Boston: Beacon, 2013, Kindle edition.
35. Quoted in "How Not to React When Your Child Tells You That He's Gay," YouTube, August 27, 2014. https://www.youtube.com/watch?v=1df_i26wh-w.
36. Margot Spencer, comment on "How Not to React When Your Child Tells You That He's Gay," YouTube, April 2015. https://www.youtube.com/watch?v=1df_i26wh-w.
37. Quoted in Cavan Sieczkowski, "Gay Teen Kicked Out of Home Diverts Donations to Homeless Shelter," *Huffington Post*, September 5, 2014. www.huffingtonpost.com.
38. Quoted in *Huffington Post*, "Caitlin Ryan's Story from the Let Love Define Family Series."
39. Quoted in *Huffington Post*, "Caitlin Ryan's Story from the Let Love Define Family Series."
40. Gay, Lesbian & Straight Education Network, *The 2013 National School Climate Survey*, www.glsen.org, 2013. http://www.slj.com/wp-content/uploads/2014/10/2013-National-School-Climate-Survey-Full-Report.pdf.
41. Austin Wallis, "Be the Change: Gay Rights," YouTube, February 1, 2015. https://www.youtube.com/watch?v=TFrt1KrTiOg.
42. Quoted in Mitch Kellaway, "Subjected to 'Constant' Bullying, California Trans Teen Dies by Suicide," *Advocate.Com*, April 9, 2015. www.advocate.com.
43. Greta Martela, "Op-Ed: Ignoring Trans Suicide Is Not 'Responsible Reporting.'" *Advocate.Com*, March 17, 2015. www.advocate.com.

How Can Teens Get Help with LGBT Issues?

44. Kathy Belge and Marke Bieschke, *Queer: The Ultimate LGBT Guide for Teens*. San Francisco: Zest, 2011. Kindle edition.
45. Belge and Bieschke. *Queer: The Ultimate LGBT Guide for Teens.*
46. ACLU, "LGBT High School Students," 2015. www.aclu.org.
47. Quoted in A.J. Trager, "Federal Government Backs Trans Youth in School Lawsuit," PrideSource, February 25, 2015. www.pridesource.com.

48. Margaret Nichols, "LGBT Youth Suicide: As Serious as It Is Preventable," Good Therapy.org, September 16, 2013. www.goodtherapy.org.

49. GLSEN, "GLSEN's Safe Space Kit: Be an Ally to LGBT Youth!," 2012. http://glsen .org.

50. GLSEN Day of Silence, "Frequently Asked Questions," 2015. www.dayofsilence.org.

51. Quoted in Andrew Seaman, "It Does Get Better for LGBT and Questioning Youth," Henrietta Hudson, January 10, 2015. http://henriettahudson.com.

List of Illustrations

Index

About the Author

Christine Wilcox writes fiction and nonfiction for young adults and adults. She has worked as an editor, an instructional designer, and a writing instructor. She lives in Richmond, Virginia, with her husband, David, and her son, Doug.